ARTIA

LEOŠ JANÁČEK

To the Memory of My Parents

The Author

LEOŠ JANÁČEK

LETTERS
AND REMINISCENCES

BOHUMÍR ŠTĚDROŇ

Translated from the Czech by
Geraldine Thomsen

1955
Artia—Prague

INTRODUCTION

This selection of letters, documents and reminiscences, drawn mainly from the Janáček Archives at the Moravian Museum in Brno, endeavours to bring Janáček's personality as close as possible to the reader. It strives to show, on a scientific basis, the life of a genius in all its manifold aspects, its creative strength and the fire of youth, prolonged to old age. The book sets out to create a better understanding of the work of Janáček and to increase the love and respect for this great Czech artist.

In our selection we can scarcely hope to encompass such a rich and full life; a music teacher, historian, conductor, composer, author, critic, ethnographist, organizer, lecturer, director of an organ school and professor of the master class in composition at the State Conservatoire, and an all-round, erudite artist. We have at our disposal typical documents from Janáček's life and work. Both life and work went always hand in hand. What Janáček was as a person, and his way of speaking, he expressed also in music: in abbreviations, in aphorisms. Take for example his style in the article which he wrote in 1923 after his visit to the International Music Festival in Venice. His thoughts, his speech and his creative work were all an "abbreviation". This came naturally to him.

This trait was certainly influenced by his native dialect, which is pronounced in a clipped manner, as if the words were being chopped off with a knife—as it is spoken in Lachia, in the Ostrava district on the border of Moravia and Silesia—in that region of Hukvaldy, where he was born on the 3rd July 1854. And still more was his artistic development influenced by his revolutionary nature, by his dissatisfaction with every form of rule and dry dogma and by his desire for truth and for freedom.

While still a student at the Prague School of Organists he defended his independence and his personality. He was forever asking why the teachers held certain opinions instead of certain others. At the entrance examination he was asked to resolve the dominant seventh chord of C major. Instead of making the leading-note rise and the seventh fall etc., he produced the following modulation:

This may be considered as the first germ of Janáček's modulations and his theoretical research. At the organ school in Prague he did not hesitate to oppose himself to the erudite theoretician František Zdeněk Skuherský, whose rendering of the Georgian Mass with its disjointed choir did not satisfy him. He declared this openly in a criticism which he did not hesitate to publish, although he was Skuherský's pupil. As a result he had to leave the school, but fortunately Skuherský let himself be persuaded by a mediator and Janáček was allowed to continue and finish his studies.

This attitude of an incorruptible revolutionary remained Janáček's characteristic during his whole life. He was married to Zdenka Schulz (1881), the daughter of his superior, who was the director of the Teachers' Training Institute, and very pro—Austrian. Later he parted with his wife, and regained her sympathies only after much trouble. His father-in-law even took disciplinary action against him, denouncing him as being of such fanatical

8

nationalism, that it bordered on madness. Thanks to a sensible inspector, the strife ended with a reconciliation and Janáček was not transferred away from Brno.

These quarrels left in him a permanent thorn against his wife and her family, and the wound never healed. As long as Janáček's beautiful and talented daughter, Olga, lived, she was the link that held the family together. After her death in 1903 the family ties became weaker. There was never any definite separation, but Janáček found a faithful friend in Mrs. Kamila Stössel. Their friendship lasted eleven years (from 1917 to 1928) and Janáček in his will refered to Mrs. Stössel as his honorary wife.

His indomitable temperament and revolutionary character manifested itself particularly at school, during his work as teacher and conductor. Always the same iconoclast, destroying old systems, old rules, seeking everywhere truth and novelty. "Write new music", he used to say to his pupils. "Learn to know truth in art, and compose sincerely in the national style." This was always Janáček's main advice when teaching at the Organ School. Here, among the pupils who wanted to do nothing but music, he felt free and more in his element than at the Teachers' Training Institute, where he had to instruct beginners in the first steps of musical theory and practice. For this reason after retiring he so willingly took on from the Teachers Training Institute the directorship and teaching at the Organ School (1904—1919) which became in 1918 the foundation of the Brno Conservatoire.

As conductor of the Brno "Beseda", of the Czech Orchestra and other societies, he gained appreciation and the praise of the critics. If it had not been for heart trouble, he would probably have reached a prominent position as a temperamental and precise conductor.

Janáček's versatile character was apparent even in his piano playing. He had intended becoming a virtuoso. In his twenty-second year he presented himself to the public as a pianist. Later he played the Rubinstein *Phantasy for two pianos*, Saint-Saëns *Piano Concerto* (1878) and Smetana's *Czech Dances*. Until 1880 his idol was Anton

Rubinstein with whom he had wanted to study in St. Petersburg in 1878, before going for a year to the Leipzig and Vienna Conservatoires. In the end he decided to concentrate on composing, where his artistic personality showed the greatest power and made him famous. Nevertheless Janáček's work as a composer was preceded by a long and tiresome preparation in the field of technique and ideas.

Janáček the composer went through four main periods: 1. The period of classical romanticism, 1872—1880, when he was dependent on Czech composers, especially Dvořák and Křížkovský.— 2. The classical folk period, 1888—1906, where he creates his individual style, based on the Moravian folk song, dance and melodic curves of speech. The culmination of this period is "Jenufa".— 3. The period of his maturity, 1906—1918, and the completion of his new style. — 4. Janáček's international acknowledgement, comprising his last intensively creative years from 1918 till 1928. All four periods have in common the interest in folk song, folk dance and the melodic curves of speech and, as a red streak passing through all his work, the social trend and his interest in mankind and in Slavonic national elements.

To his first period belong the early choral works, in particular the four male-voice choruses dedicated to Dvořák, his compositions for string orchestra *Idyll* and *Suite*, the *Romance for violin*, the *Piano variations* and the opera *Šárka* (1887). Up to the time of the completion of *Šárka* Janáček was under the influence of Dvořák's music, which partly arose from his activities as choir-master of the Brno "Beseda" and was conditioned by Dvořák's affinity to the people, by his endeavours to express Slavonic characteristics in music and by his sympathetic attitude towards the musical life of the Moravian folk. Janáček sent his first opera to Dvořák for an opinion and made several changes according to Dvořák's advice. Yet this first opera had little influence on Janáček's later development, as it was not performed until 1925, on the occasion of his 70th anniversary.

The second, the classical folk period, is the most important one for his creative development. From 1888 he made a systematic study of folk songs and dances and penetrated deeply into the dramatic and melodic structure of folk speech, a structure which he called *the melodic curves of speech*. In this he sought dramatic reality and the roots of the very expression of the human mind. He was convinced that every dramatic composer must study living speech. In the human voice and speech he saw the surest expression of the various states of mind, and the human being was in his speech to him the most perfect artist. Thus Janáček became the founder of a special theory of melodic curves of speech. Although he demanded that the melodic curves of speech be read solely according to the cadence of the notes themselves, he let himself be influenced by their suggested melody and took them for musical phrases, which could be harmonised on the basis of their special musical value. The melodic curves of speech and the Moravian folk songs had an obvious influence on his musical style. They caused his music to be abbreviated and disjointed and were the source of his dramatic effects and unusual dramatic qualities. Dvořák in vain exhorted Janáček with the words: "More melody, don't be afraid of it!" Janáček had his own melody and Dvořák failed to realise that Janáček wanted to be himself. The melodic curves of speech and the Moravian folk song were for him the basis of his style. As the Moravian song, when compared to the Czech, is looser in form and is built up rhapsodically, it presents different principles from the Czech folk songs, and this explains why Janáček differed so much in style from composers such as Smetana and Dvořák. This does not mean that they have nothing in common. Yet to seek and create an *a priori* affiliation and to graft Janáček on to the Smetana tree is damaging and unjust to Janáček. Janáček grew mainly out of Moravian song and out of his melodic curves of speech, which he evolved into a symphonic style in a progressive and national way.

The classical folk period of Janáček manifested itself in many arrangements of Moravian folk songs and dances *(Moravian Folk Poetry in Songs, Folk Dances in Moravia, Hukvaldy Folk Poetry in Songs)* and in the beautiful stylizations of his Wallachian–Lachian dances. (Wallachia and Lachia are two districts in Moravia ethnographically close to each other). Two of the dances *(Starodávný* and *Pilky)* were his first printed orchestral works (1890, op. 2.) to make Janáček known to a wider public. But unfortunately they never became as popular abroad as Dvořák's *Slavonic Dances.* Unlike Dvořák's, most of them are composed on the melodies of definite Lachian Dances, which brings them nearer to Smetana's *Czech Dances* for piano, although their orchestration reminds us more of Dvořák. The dances *Požehnaný* (No. 2) and *Čeladenský* (No. 5 in the pocket edition of the score) are most typical of the character of the music of Lachia, because of their constant repeating and interchanging of short melodic elements. They are closely linked with the Lachian dance *Troják* (which exists only in manuscript) with its rhythm of alternating $\frac{2}{4}$ and $\frac{3}{4}$ bars, known equally well from Vítězslav Novák's *Wallachian Dances.* In these folk dances, which on account of their rhythmical arrangements and their melodies, repeat themselves *ad infinitum,* as, for instance the *Troják,* and which correspond to Russian folk songs and dances, I see an important principle of Janáček's style, based on the repetition of short melodic elements. The *Lachian Dances* are also a precious document of Janáček's orchestration, although not as brilliantly colourful as those of Dvořák, but nevertheless impressive and effective. They refute all the exaggerated objections to his orchestration, which appeared during the time when *Jenufa* was being re-written. The *Lachian Dances* are the most perfect artistic result of the ethnographical enthusiasm and the revival of Moravia in the years 1889—1895, which culminated in the Ethnographical Exhibition in Prague (1895).

Janáček now proceeded to make his style and methods of expression more scientific. He made contact with the Moravian expert on dialects, František Bartoš, and took to editing the musical side of the publications of Moravian Folk Songs (published by the Czech Academy in Prague, 1901). He penetrated still deeper into their spirit. He studied their form, their melodic and harmonic components and he wrote a long treatise on Moravian folk songs. Yet even this failed to satisfy his demands for a truthful representation. Again it is with the help of the melodic curves of speech that he penetrates to the very soul of the people, finding in their words expressed by their feelings an immense reserve of dramatic and melodic expressions. He studied them everywhere, among adults and children, he noted down the songs of birds, the bubbling of streams and the rumblings of the sea and he concerned himself with the length of time which the sounds continued to vibrate. In short, the whole universe was for him one great complex of sounds.

Janáček's studies of Moravian songs and dances and his belief in the melodic curves of speech are unique in Czech music for their quantity and depth. In this field his studies on the melodic curves of speech are unparallelled. This was the source of Janáček's individual style which begins a new era in Czech music. *Jenufa is the* first great monument of Janáček's style and the completion of *Jenufa* and its production in the National Theatre in Brno (1904) is a milestone in the classical folk period of Janáček, who at the same time becomes the creator of a new dramatic style. Similarly, as in the lyrical cantata *Amarus* (1897) or the scenic cantata, *Our Father*, Janáček's compassion for the humiliated and suffering human being is given full scope for development.

The roots of *Jenufa* go back as far as the Moravian folk song, *Jealousy*, in which Janáček found a similar example of unlimited jealousy, such as we see demonstrated in the village youth, who passionately loves Jenufa. At this time he reaped the harvest of his ethnographical research. He was considered to be the first authority on Moravian folk songs. He organised the Moravian section of the All-Slav exhibition in St. Petersburg. He became chairman of the Working Committee for the preservation of folk music in Moravia and Silesia (1905) and he published books on the best methods for collecting folk songs. After Bartoš's death in 1906 he became the leading personality in the ethnographical research in Moravian folk music, which remained the deepest source of his inspiration throughout his whole life.

In the third period of his creative activity Janáček led a great struggle for the recognition of *Jenufa*, which signifies the culmination of his efforts for the enlightenment of mankind, and of his love for the Slavonic nations and for Russia in particular. Janáček met with great misunderstanding of his new operatic style. For fully twelve years he struggled to have *Jenufa* performed at the National Theatre in Prague, because the Brno Opera House lacked space on its small stage and did not possess a full cast. The re-writing of *Jenufa* from the point of view of direction and dramatic compactness, did not satisfy the Prague theatre and Janáček finally agreed to the changes in the orchestration, which were made by the director of the Prague opera, Karel Kovařovic. The first performance of *Jenufa* in Prague in 1916 was the beginning of Janáček's success at home and abroad.

His social and national subjects were drawn from events in Brno, from the works of Petr Bezruč and from Russian literature. At the beginning of the 20th century there were great internal conflicts between the ruling German bourgeoisie and the Czech townsfolk, together with the oppressed working people. In 1905, during the manifestations for the founding of a Czech university in Brno, demonstrations were held which led to the death of two workers. Janáček was the only artist who reacted to this incident, which he did by writing a cycle of piano pieces. Shortly afterwards he was completely captivated by the revolutionary poetry of Petr Bezruč whose *Silesian Songs* expressed with such penetration the social and national opression in the Těšín district. With his choruses, composed to Bezruč's poems (*Kantor Halfar*, *Maryčka Magdonová* and the *70.000*), Janáček became a brilliant counterpart of the poet. He gave to his choruses dramatic strength and power of such effect, that his choral works, thanks to the Moravian Teachers Choir conducted by Ferdinad Vach, made him known both at home and abroad long before *Jenufa* had been produced. In these choruses Janáček's struggle against oppression, misery, humiliation and loss of national identity reached its culmination. The orchestral ballad, *The Fiddler's Child* (1912), is equally concerned with social questions, and the cantata, *Everlasting Gospel* (1914), proclaims his love for all mankind on the eve of the first World War.

The *Excursions of Mr. Brouček to the XVth Century and to the Moon* (1917) and the orchestral rhapsody, *Taras Bulba* (1918), composed after a story by Gogol, are an echo of the tragedy of war, sounded at a time when Janáček firmly believed in the victory of Czech independence. That is why in the *Excursions of Mr. Brouček to the XVth Century* he used Hussite motives and the famous song of the Hussite warriors. That is also why he attacked the faint-heartedness of the petty bourgeoisie and was convinced that "no fire nor torture can be found which would be sufficient to destroy the strength of the Russian people" (Taras Bulba).

Janáček's time was ripe only after 1918, when the Czechoslovak Republic had been proclaimed. He remained faithful to his original principles and ideas, but concentrated more and more on operatic works. The operas *Kata Kabanová*, *Fox Sharpears*, *Macropulos Secret* and *The House of the Dead* demonstrate an exceptional creative strength and intensive activity, enabling the seventy-year-old composer to give the world in quick succession new works of art. He used to compare the first performance of his operas in Brno to the first performance of Smetana's works from the point of view of their importance and the repercussions they caused. Of all the honours and invitations from abroad, as for instance to England in 1926, he had received, he gained the greatest satisfaction from his honorary doctorate of the Masaryk University in Brno (1925) because he had always striven for a scientific basis to his work. During that period Janáček found a sympathetic friend in a young lady, to whom he used to confide his artistic plans. From this union issued the *Diary of One who Vanished* and *Intimate Letters*. With this second String Quartet and with the collective opera *The House of the Dead* after Dostoevsky, Janáček bade farewell in his work to mankind.

All this I have endeavoured to demonstrate with the letters and reminiscences of this book. Janáček fought for his new style as much with words as with music. We will see in his letters how often his music was misunderstood, although he continued to declare the fact that he did not merely play about with notes, but that

15

he dipped his music in nature and life. In the letters we see his steady growth into a responsible artist, who, from a village schoolmaster's son, became the foremost composer of his country. We shall see how constantly he followed the truths in which he believed and with what perseverance he created not only works of introspective character, but also works which proved faithfulness to the people and the maxims of social and national freedom.

In the following pages may be seen Janáček's great human qualities: his love of mankind, his freedom and dignity, his artistic greatness, his faith in the high mission of art and his indomitable and fighting spirit. These qualities crystallised while he was composing *Jenufa*, the work of his pain, love and fame.

After the victorious struggle for *Jenufa*, Janáček's ideas were accepted and he was able to teach his pupils the maxims that led him to his achievements:

"Grow out of your innermost selves
Never renounce your opinions
Do not toil for recognition
But always do all you can
So that the field alloted to you
May prosper."

Bohumír Štědroň.

Brno, the year of the 100th aniversary of Janáček's birth, 1954.

1. The school in Hukvaldy, where Janáček was born.

2. Facsimile of a page from the choral arrangement of a Hukvaldy song.

1. JANÁČEK IS BORN

Certified to be a true copy of an entry in the local register of births and baptisms, page 145, according to which a son was born in wedlock on July 3rd 1854 at No. 40, in the village of Hukvaldy, and baptised on July 4th 1854 in the village church of Our Lord and St. Maxmilian the martyr

Janáček, Leo Eugen

Father: *Janáček Jiří, school-master of Hukvaldy.*

Mother: *Amalia, daughter of Karel Grulich, draper of Příbor and his wife, Kateřina, née Wiesnar of Příbor.*

Baptised by: *Father Vincenc Zatloukal, castle chaplain.*

Godparents: *Vincenc Janáček, school-master of Albrechtičky, Rosalie, his wife.*

Birth certificate from the Roman Catholic vicarage of Rychaltice near Hukvaldy. *Adolf Kubis* gave the above certificate in an article on the Janáček family published on the 2nd June 1929 in the paper *Lidové Noviny*. The original is in German. — *Hukvaldy No. 40*, where Janáček was born, is the school building and stands close to the Archbishop's country house which is overlooked by the ruins of Hukvaldy castle. The family living-room is marked by a plaque designed by the sculptor, Julius Pelikán, of Olomouc. — In the register, the family tree on the father's side is incomplete. — Leoš's godfather, *Vincenc Janáček*, was the brother of Leoš's father. — *Adolf Kubis*, born 1876 in Brušperk near Moravská Ostrava, a patriot and publicist.

2. HIS GRANDMOTHER

Leoš's grandmother, Anna, was the pillar of the Janáček family. With her quiet, calm personality and her love she protected Leoš from the severity and hot temper of his father. She brought up and educated healthy children, helped by her economy, self-sacrifice and untiring industriousness. She bore her children's troubles on her own shoulders, and her silent presence was the means of saving them from being too severely dealt with for small offences.

The author of this recollection, *Vincenc Janáček* (1821—1901), Leoš's uncle, succeded Jiří Janáček as schoolmaster of Albrechtičky. In 1897, during a holiday at Kateřinky near Opava, he wrote his important "*Life of Jiří Janáček*" from which the above is taken.

3. HIS FATHER AS THE TEACHER OF PAVEL KŘÍŽKOVSKÝ

Jiří, Leoš's father (born 1815 in Albrechtičky, died 1866 in Hukvaldy), was the fifth child and third son of his father, also called Jiří. He had a hard and eventful life, and made his way with difficulty. His father insisted that in order to prepare himself properly for his teaching career, it was necessary to know something of music. For this reason before finishing his studies, he was sent to the rector of Velký Petřvald, Josef Richter, whom he knew to be a good organist. From Petřvald he was sent in 1831 to the main school of Příbor (run by Piarist monks) for his preparatory course, and served a term as an assistant teacher. At the age of sixteen he began teaching at Neplachovice near Opava.

"There the little orphan, Pavel Křížkovský, became attached to him. Křížkovský's mother had begged Jiří Janáček to give her son a musical training. This he did and later installed him in the church school of the Holy Ghost in Opava, and so helped him to the beginnings of his activities as a composer. Křížkovský afterwards repaid these services to Janáček's son Leoš in Brno."

Vincenc Janáček: "Life of Jiří Janáček". – Pavel Křížkovský (1820–1885), Czech composer of much choral music in folk-song style. Attended the Neplachovice school near Opava, from 1826 to 1832, where, during his last years, he was discoverd by the teacher, Jiří Janáček, Leoš's father, who cared for the orphan and helped him to be accepted as a choir-boy at Opava.

4. HIS FATHER AS CHOIR MASTER

The arrival of Jiří Janáček, Leoš's father, in Hukvaldy in 1848, was of major consequence to the future history of the family. From that time on, the fates of Hukvaldy and of the Janáček family take the same course. The small parish at the foot of the castle hill began to play an important part in the cultural chronicles of Moravia, not only as the birthplace of Leoš Janáček, but also as the place to which the composer turned in his search for rest and further inspiration. Hukvaldy was his second home. Jiří Janáček had fourteen children of which nine lived to grow up. He inherited from his father an unusual teaching ability, a love of gardening and a fiery temper. He was, like so many of the Janáčeks, explosive but, nevertheless, persevering. At the beginning of the year 1865, he inaugurated a reading and singing club of which he was the first choir-master.

"Modest Hukvaldy thus outdid in song and in national consciousness the towns, both large and small, by encouraging with the help of music, brotherhood, patriotism and a love of their homeland."

(Quotation from the Brno daily paper, *Moravská orlice*, 29th September 1865).

5. JANÁČEK AS CHOIR BOY

"My father used to be invited to visit the neighbouring parishes with his music, even the rich parish of Rychaltice. We children used to go trudging along with him. I was the descant, my sister played the viola; altogether we made a full choir of singers and players——— At Rychaltice there were collapsible music stands and a gilded organ ornamented with acanthus on both sides of the keyboard and at the back, close to the window, were two enormous drums as big as flour-bins — tympani. This musical entertaining among the schoolmasters lasted until about the year 1863, when the two rectors fell out over a trifle which put an end to the visits to Rychaltice. High mass took place only on special holidays."

Excerpt from Janáček's autobiography edited by *Adolf Veselý* under the title "*Life and Work of Leoš Janáček*". — *Adolf Veselý*, born 1886, Czech author and journalist, was in contact with Janáček at the time when Veselý was on the newspaper *Lidové Noviny* 1919—1925, a Czech daily, which came out in Brno. — *The rector of Rychaltice*, with whom Jiří Janáček played, was called Jan Valentin Hlacík. — *Rychaltice*, a small village near Hukvaldy.

6. JANÁČEK EXTOLS HIS BIRTHPLACE

As you can see from the postcard, it is more beautiful here than at Luhačovice. Here is real peace. Round the castle there is a park containing a herd of fallow-deer.

They allow you to approach within a few steps. They have antlers like spades. The park also has a stud-farm, with a herd of sixty Andalusian ponies, grazing at will. Paths which take hours to walk along, well kept; and benches for resting. On the second postcard you see the parish. The food situation here is difficult, but not too bad. My sister and I have five litres of milk a day; a litre costs ninety hellers. Part of it has to be churned into butter. New potatoes cost one crown a kilo, a chicken for roasting costs 10 crowns. Mushrooms can be had for the picking. Meat has to be ordered from the nearby town of Místek. I hope that the brewery, the oldest in Moravia, will let me have some of the real stuff.

Walks to the castle and a rest at the top (it isn't too high) are magnificent. The sun, when it comes out, warms as though it was nearer. And the air! It smells of raisins. If I had any power over you, I would immediately bring you here for your health. The drinking water comes from a spring, which they call "consecrated".

Round the castle there flows a mountain stream, the Ondřejnice; I hope to get acquainted with the trout that dart about in its waters. There will be plenty of fruit. It is raining on the grain which is not yet mown. The gamekeeper cut a cabbage and brought it in; when cleaned, it weighed seven kilos.

Hukvaldy near Příbor, 5th August 1918.

Leoš Janáček.

Leoš Janáček describes the beauty of his birthplace in a letter to his friend *Mrs. Kamila Stössel* (1892—1935), in which he invites her to Hukvaldy. — At the time of World War I it was only natural that the food problem would be of interest.

7. IN PRAISE OF HUKVALDY

Walks over land as flat as a pancake or over gentle slopes; well kept paths, benches for resting. An old castle on the hill top, below the tidy parish. And the forest all around. Lime trees, some of which are five hundred years old. The oldest brewery and a farm where there are about two hundred cows. No shortage of milk. During August there are plenty of vegetables good enough to be shown in a horticultural show.

I am not praising it because I have the freedom of the parish, nor because it is my birthplace, but because I have never known a tidier, more healthy place with stronger air and brighter sunshine. Here I have found peace. I work a little and in the evening I sit under my lime tree and gaze into the forest until nightfall. Silence falls from each tree to the ground. The cock wakes me in the morning. His is such a strange melody that I have not yet succeeded in taking it down.

From Janáček's letters to *Mrs. Stössel*, Hukvaldy, 10th August 1918. – Janáček was given the freedom of Hukvaldy in 1916.

8. STUDIES WITH PAVEL KŘÍŽKOVSKÝ

It was certainly not by chance that I became a musician: my entire surroundings! When I was eight, it was said of me: "The boy will outdo his father." I went to Brno when I was eleven. There I found Křížkovský. I never miss a chance of playing the organ, and Křížkovský once said: "Listen to him, he already knows the main theme of the mass which we are going to perform." I simply had it in me from the cradle. And then there was the choir of the old Brno monastery—well, as I said, I was surrounded by it.

From an interview with Leoš Janáček published in the paper *Literární svět* on the 8th March 1928.

9. AT THE OLD BRNO CLOISTER FOUNDATION

Blue boys! That was the name by which we boys of the Thurn-Vallsassina foundation were known throughout Brno because of our pale blue, white bordered uniforms. Neglected but guarded; in moments of loneliness we looked out of the barred windows. From the Prelate's garden, the birds flew for the crumbs which we threw to them. Small blue birds, blue as well, but freer than our kind.

Every day we practised singing and piano playing, as well as our own particular instruments. There was also quartet and ensemble practice. The wind-instrument players helped each other out with technical problems. We had an old tradition to live up to. The "Blues" were known all over Brno. Their music was welcome at concerts given for ministers and other potentates. They lent a hand in the theatre orchestra; no church choir could do without their help. They even played at aristocratic balls and were brought daily into the refectory after the roast had been served. Every day at table and every Sunday at Divine Service—and many more occasions! It is the more amazing when you consider that each "Blue" was either a student of philosophy or logic or a pupil attending the grammar or ordinary class where it was also necessary to study diligently. The time-table of practice and lessons had to be kept to. There were rehearsals which were in reality public concerts. The institution had its own teachers, its own prefects, a conductor and the director—from the year 1853, no other than Pavel Kříž-kovský.

Leoš Janáček. – From *Adolf Veselý's* book. – *The Foundation of Countess Sibylla Polixena of Montani,* neé Countess Thurn–Vallsassina, was attached to the Augustine monastery of Old Brno, founded in 1648. This Foundation was the forerunner of the Brno Conservatoire.

10. FIRST ATTEMPTS AT COMPOSING

When attending the Old Brno monastery Foundation, Janáček wore his hair in long curls, which touched his shoulders. On his head, a flat cap and on his feet, high felt boots. In this way he trudged daily to the institute, his music books tucked under his arm. He was already an excellent pianist and in the monastery he found a fellow pupil of equal talent. These two, under the guidance of the great Křížkovský, played Beethoven symphonies together. They were rare moments of artistic enjoyment, whenever the two enthusiasts sat down to the piano. It was probably at this time that Janáček first felt the urge to compose. At that time he wrote some simple songs, one of which he remembers to this day. These songs were written on special coloured paper: blue, pink and other colours. He ruled the lines himself and carefully copied out the music. The song runs:

> If you do not like me
> What does it matter?
> I'll walk to the hill-top
> And find me a better . . .

It was a nice song and both of us were immensely pleased with it. It had in fact really turned out very well. When I especially commended the passage "what does it matter?" his face brightened, and I see him as if it were today playing the accompaniment with illustrative gestures. His eyes would shine—yes, really shine. They were among the first happy moments of life.

By František Neumann. — The historian Father Alois Augustin Neumann (1892—1948) published a history of the Neumann family among which were the memoirs of his uncle František Neumann, who lived with Janáček at the Foundation for five years.

11. PAVEL KŘÍŽKOVSKÝ AS CONDUCTOR

Pavel Křížkovský was an excellent conductor. No work which he rehearsed was ever forgotten by anyone who played or sang under him. No one could penetrate more deeply or boldly or with greater perspicacity into the spirit of the works of other composers. Forgive me, if I give here a little picture of the monastery choir where his baton reigned supreme. Today I can still hear the section of the Creed in the D minor mass of Michael Haydn. I see Křížkovský, frowning deeply and glaring over his spectacles at Mr. Hönig, our double-bass player. Poor Mr. Hönig could not do justice either to Michael Haydn or Křížkovský, especially if even the organist Mr. Hanáček, who was head-teacher of the town school of Old Brno, an impassioned musician and copyist of Haydn's choir, could not come off his note because of a broken pedal. Father Barosch, a well known player and much sought-after teacher of the violin in Brno, had to have his fiddle carried to the choir. Mr. Rudiš had to have his favourite violin tuned for him. Both were first violins in the choir. On ordinary Sundays, the orchestra was sadly lacking in numbers, and the same must be said for the wind instruments: oboes and trombones played only on special holidays. On the other hand we choristers, well in the front at the left side of the choir, we were a group of reliable singers. Our voices, from daily practice, were tuneful and certainly as clear as flutes: to conduct us—it was quite unnecessary. We kept our eyes fixed in front of us but our ears were strained backwards. We were pleased when, on special Sundays, we heard Mr. Štross "weaving" away on his oboe. On these occasions Křížkovský did not conduct, but played the viola standing on a pedestal. Sometimes we had guests in the choir. On special days and at Easter, Miss Hřímalá, sister of the composer, sang soprano solos. Mr. Pěta had a pleasing tenor: we were delighted when we were sent to him with the message that he should come to sing and stay on afterwards to lunch. Yes, we certainly sang to the Glory of God, but also for our own pleasure. Even the shorter mass by Beethoven was given.

Then there came the so-called reform in church music. Křížkovský, who in the beginning was very loath to take up with the reform, was the first to study and perform Greith's Mass in E major. Křížkovský was later transfered to Olomouc from where he used to visit us to see how we progressed "under my direction."

Part of Janáček's memoirs which he published in an article *The significance of Pavel Křížkovský for Moravian folk music and for Czech music generally*. (Český lid No. XI, 1902, pp. 257—263). — *Michael Haydn* (1737—1806), brother of Josef Haydn, renowned for his church music which was much played in Bohemia. — *Karl Greith* (1828—1887), a succesful composer of church music. — Karel Eichler gives more details about the choir musicians in his biography of Pavel Křížkovský. (Brno 1904), p. 13.

12. JANÁČEK TO STUDY IN PRAGUE

With reference to the application of Mr. Lev Janáček, I am pleased to state my opinion that his musical gifts, especially for organ playing, are exceptionally outstanding and that, given a full opportunity of studying music thoroughly, he will, one day, become a really distinguished musician. His unusual talent fully justifies such hopes.

Pavel Křížkovský, choir master.

Brno, 12th January 1874.

Pavel Křížkovský's recommendation for the admittance of Janáček into the Prague School of Organists.

13. HIS POVERTY AS A STUDENT

With a piece of chalk, I drew the piano key-board on the table, and in this way my fingers learned to play the notes of Bach's *Preludes and Fugues*. It was painful, I was dying for the living sounds. Hire a piano? Where would I get the money? But one day, goodness knows where it came from, there was a piano standing in my room in Štěpánská Street. This miracle I ascribed to Mr. Ferdinand Lehner, first chaplain of Karlín church and editor of the *Cyril*. A malicious smile played about his good natured face. At the end of the school year, the piano disappeared unobtrusively from my room.

And how often he took my hungry self out to a good dinner. Lunch at the Konvikt restaurant cost 25 *kreuzers*. My landlady gave me breakfast free. Heating in winter? I used surreptitiously to open the door of the neighbouring room from where a little heat would steal through.

Extract from Janáček's autobiography (publ. 1924). A document describing the poverty and hunger of the young composer. – *Ferdinand Lehner* (1837—1914), Czech writer on music and editor of the magazine *Cyril*. Janáček studied at the Prague School of organists from 1874 to 1875. His teachers were *František Blažek* (1815—1908), and the particularly thorough theoretician, *František Zdeněk Skuherský* (1830—1892).

14. AT A CONCERT OF SMETANA'S WORKS

My memories of Bedřich Smetana are like a picture of how children imagine God: in the clouds. It was at a concert on the Žofín island in what was for Smetana the fateful year, 1874. I was standing near the orchestra. His work came to an end, and a deafening storm of applause broke out, culminating in shouts of "Smetana". Suddenly there was such a shuffling and pushing all round me that I seemed to be in darkness. The afflicted composer was being led up the steps. His face impressed itself into my soul. I can still see it clearly; but always as through a mist. Certainly my eyes devoured him, — for all else, I was completely deaf and blind.

At the time when Janáček was studying in Prague, Smetana was smitten with incurable deafness. Janáček saw him appear at the concert, and the expression of sorrow and suffering on the older composer's face was deeply engraved into Janáček's memory. However, it was 25 years after Smetana's death that Janáček first made public this impression in the magazine *Dalibor* (No. XXXI 1909 p. 258). He later restated this impression in the magazine *Hudební Besídka* (No. I, 1924—1925, p. 807). According to Helfert's book on Janáček (p. 101), this event took place at the Smetana benefit concert of 4th April 1875, when the symphonic poems *Vyšehrad* and *Vltava* were performed for the first time.

15. JANÁČEK'S ARTISTIC TALENTS

The Directorate of the Royal Imperial Slavonic Teachers Training Institute

Brno.

In reply to your letter, dated 19th April 1877 Ref. No. 123, I have the honour to say that it gives me the greatest pleasure to state my opinion of the musical abilities of Professor Leoš Janáček in the warmest possible terms. It is my firm belief that Janáček is an artist of real worth; he possesses all the qualities necessary for attaining the highest ideals in art, namely: talent, intelligence, perseverance and enthusiasm. Therefore Janáček is already showing striking progress both as composer and performer. He possesses extensive knowledge of musical literature, a subtle ear and rich understanding of musical theory and aesthetics, which give him the right to activities as conductor and critic. He has given proof of this on many occasions on the concert platform.

Under these favourable circumstances, I allow myself to express the wish that the authorities in charge will see fit to afford Janáček's unusual talents every opportunity for their further development.

Prague, 12th April 1878.   *František Zdeněk Skuherský,*
Director of the School of organists.

František Zdeněk Skuherský, Janáček's teacher at the school of organists, sent his opinion of Janáček to the director of the Brno institute of teachers, *Emilian Schulz,* on receiving Janáček's request for leave to study at the Leipzig Conservatoire.

16. AT THE TEACHERS TRAINING INSTITUTE IN BRNO

The State Institute of male teachers in Brno had, from its inauguration, many professors of outstanding personality and ability, not only in literature but especially in music. The music teachers included many excellent artists the foremost being Leoš Janáček and later Professor Ferdinand Vach. Leoš Janáček was the first teacher of the newly set up Slavonic Teachers' Training Institute (1871) which was at that time housed in the Minorite Monastery. In him the Institute possessed a musical genius such as they had never had and are not likely ever to have. Janáček's teaching activities at the Institute began under the directorship of his future father-in-law, Emilian Schulz, in the year 1872, and ended at the beginning of November, 1903, when Janáček was given a year's leave on account of his health. He was officially given indefinitive leave at the end of October, 1904.

From Štědroň's article, *Leoš Janáček at the Male Teachers' Institute in Brno,* in the magazine *Tempo,* (No. XIII, 1933—1934, pp. 315 ff.). — Dr *Bohumír Štědroň,* lecturer of the Masaryk University in Brno, author of the present book. — *Ferdinand Vach* (1860—1939), outstanding Czech choirmaster, founder of the Moravian Teacher's choir and reformer of choral singing.

17. WITHOUT THE RIGHT TO A SALARY

Decree of the Royal Imperial Provincial Council of Schools, 25th November, 1872, No. 24—171, by which the candidate, Leo Janáček, is admitted to the teaching staff as an assistant teacher of the preparatory school, provisionally without the right to a salary.

Ministerial decree of the 12th April, 1876, No. 5429, authorising the appointment of a music teacher to the Institute of Teachers in Brno, who is to be responsible for the supervision of the teaching of music at the beforementioned Institute; if desirable, to give lessons in that subject. Ministerial decree of the 14th May, 1880, No. 3543, by which the assistant teacher of music, Leo Janáčck, is made a full teacher of music.

First report of the Royal Imperial Czech Teachers' Training Institute from the year 1871—1872 to the year 1896—1897 (pp. 41, 46, and 57). — Janáček became a teacher at the Institute in his 18th year. His artistic gifts, the directorship of the old Brno choir in place of Křížkovský, who had been transferred to Olomouc, and the kind help of the director of the Institute, Emilian Schulz, secured an anchorage in Brno for the young composer. He also taught in the Royal Imperial Slavonic Teachers' Training Institute from 1876 to 1878.

18. OBLIGED TO TEACH BEGINNERS

I knew him as professor of music at the Teachers' Institute in Brno. At that time, he had not yet reached the peak of his fame, although he was obviously an outstanding figure among the teachers. All his pupils were aware of this. Even if our teacher was unusually silent, reserved and strict in every way, we always welcomed him with unusual respect whenever he entered the music room. With his characteristic shaky tread, he shuffled his small person round our benches and, without a word, sat down to the piano, his shock of black wavy hair gleaming in the sunlight. Then we felt as though we were in another atmosphere, a truly artistic one, where the soul triumphed over matter. And when we sang folk-songs from the Bartoš—Janáček *Bouquet* and the master himself accompanied us, it was evident to us all that a rare artist stood before us whom, however, not everyone understood.

After a longer period of contact with our teacher, we came to understand his rather unusual attitude to his pupils. His singing lessons—I am not speaking of his music lessons in general—became holidays of the spirit to which we looked forward more and more as time went on. What were his lessons, especially his violin lessons like? He himself, unflatteringly, expressed his opinion of them on one occasion when he asked me, as Professor of Music at the Teachers' Institute in Brno, what I thought of my profession. He said: "For me it is torture!". Now, from my own experience, I understand the full meaning of Janáček's drastic words. I see him, as though it were today, with what unwillingness he climbed onto the conductor's rostrum in the music room in order to conduct such works as Pleyel's duets. Then, to be obliged to listen to those forty indifferent violinists playing on various kinds of fiddles with varying degrees of skill or, rather, lack of skill — that was indeed torture for a master of tone and musical composition. And this applied to his organ lessons, and probably also to his piano lessons: not to mention his lessons in the theory of music, although there he could at least expound his theories which were then still unrecognized.

Taken from *Josef Černík's* article *Memories of Leoš Janáček* which appeared in *Lidové Noviny*, 12th August, 1933. – *Josef Černík*, born 1880, Brno, composer. Studied in the Brno Teachers' Institute from 1898 to 1900 and at the School of Organists under Janáček from 1904 to 1905. From 1921 to 1926 he was Professor of music at the Brno Institute of Teachers. – *František Bartoš* (1837—1906), collected folk-songs, specialist in Moravian folk art. Produced, in collaboration with Janáček, *A Bouquet of Moravian Folk-Songs*. (Published by Emil Šolc in Telč in 1890, 1892 and 1901.) The latest edition (the 4th) appeared in Prague in 1953.) *Ignác Josef Pleyel* (1752—1831), German composer of popular violin duets.

19. DISCIPLINE IN CHOIR SINGING

Leoš Janáček, when a singing teacher at the Old Brno Grammar School, was known for his great kindness. Whoever saw his charming smile or the kind expression in his eyes, never forgot them. He had, however, a fiery temper, was irritable and liable to fits of uncontrollable anger. If anyone in the choir made a mistake, Janáček knew immediately which unfortunate creature had sung the wrong note, and pounced on him with baton or pencil, both of which were equally dangerous weapons in his hands. But we soon accustomed ourselves to such treatment, and even became proud of it. "I say! He jolly well went for me today!" "Did you see how his baton bounced off my skull!"–We boasted about our rough treatment.

Leoš Janáček was never one of those teachers who make entries in class-books or who send in complaints to the director. He dealt with us on the spot with his baton or pencil or scores, and with severe and vigorous scoldings which invariably began "Yah, you good-for-nothing!" But we were fond of him. You know how it is; a rebuke from the master, a rebuke from the director, then punishment and a bad mark for behaviour. Adherence to the normal system of punishment in schools was entirely unknown with Janáček. I was in the 4th class, when he gave up his post, to be replaced by Emanuel Vach. We were sorry to part with him and each one of us begged him to sign our autograph books.

From the article by *Vladimír Sís* entitled *Professor Leoš Janáček*, which appeared in *Národní listy* 15th August 1940. – *Emanuel Vach* (1866–1936) was, from the year 1898, Professor of Music in Brno. He taught at the Institute of Women Teachers from 1902–1912, and succeeded Janáček at the Old Brno Grammar School. He was a brother of the well-known conductor of the Moravian Teacher's choir, Ferdinand Vach.

20. EMPHASIS ON FOLK SONG

Whether at the Institute of Teachers or at the Old Brno Grammar School, or later at the School of organists, Janáček's pupils were made to understand that the basis of all true art of any lasting value is conscientious hard work. At the Institute of Teachers Janáček paid special attention to singing, which he taught according to the Pivoda method. He devoted much time to songs and choral works and attached great importance to the singing of folk songs which he chose mainly from the Bartoš—Janáček *Bouquet of Moravian Folk Songs*, to which he added his own inimitable piano accompaniments. He made a special point of instilling his enthusiastic love of folksongs and of children into each candidate teacher. Thus Janáček, a teacher from a family of teachers, is the consummation of a long line of teachers, teacher-patriots and musicians. He is their greatest representative and a real genius among them.

From Štědroň's article, *Leoš Janáček and the Institute of Male Teachers in Brno.* (*Tempo*, 1933—34, No. XIII, pp. 315 ff.) — *František Pivoda* (1824—1898), singing teacher of Prague; published in 1883, his *New Method of Teaching Singing*, which contained wall maps and diagrams.

21. A YEAR'S LEAVE TO STUDY ABROAD

Ministerial decree of the 17th July, 1877, No. 10,800, in which leave of absence is given to Leoš Janáček for the first quarter of the year 1879—1880, in order that he may continue his studies in music at the higher institutions of Leipzig and Vienna.

Ministerial decree of the 18th January, 1880, No. 260, in which leave is given to the teacher Leoš Janáček until the end of the year 1879—1880.

First report of the Royal Imperial Czech Teachers' Institute in Brno, pp. 55, 57. — Janáček studied at the Conservatoire from October, 1879, till the end of February, 1880. In Vienna he continued his studies from April, 1880, till June of the same year.

3. Leoš Janáček (about 1882).

4. The Organ School at Brno, to-day the Leoš Janáček Museum.

22. JANÁČEK TO HIS FIANCÉE

My dearest Zdenči!

Is it not true, my dearest Zdenči, that only love which enobles us is true love? I am so happy that I love you — but it gives me no peace. I used to feel so lonely and indifferent to life. In one of those hours of depression, which used to occur so often, it was enough for me to look at your picture and my ugly mood retreated like malicious spirits before an angel. The time of my falling in love with you begins the overthrow of my former self, which is now being played out in my soul. Now the process is quickening because I am thrown back entirely on myself. It is an unending struggle and fight between my old self and that which I want to become, and to which I feel I will win through with your help.

If I had never known you, I would have become an ordinary musician, perhaps slightly above the average, but entirely without moral support. Before I knew you I had tendencies which threatened to become my downfall. Now, I see in you an angel. I know I must love you and I have settled accounts with myself, with my plans and with my almost negative outlook on life and on humanity. There have been moments when my former moods appeared and I became afraid of myself. But I banished the fear with my great desire to improve. I would not ask your help if I had doubts about my ability to change radically for the better. I am so happy that I must make the decision to become a genuine person who will act only in such a way as to be worthy of you. Also, I shall hope to become a greater artist than would otherwise have been possible. In later years my conscience would have hindered my work.

I beg of you to love me, my dearest Zdenči. Your love maintains me. I believe only in you. I have written down my thoughts in this way so as not to conceal the least detail from you. I want you to rule me. My only happiness is the thought that we will

our lives together and that, for you, I will be able to
ood.

From a letter written on October 31st, 1878, from Leipzig by Janáček to *Zdenka Schulz*
the daughter of the director of the Teachers' Institute, where he was employed. In it he ardently
assures her of his love, but also reveals to her the inner conflict between his old self and the
better person he hopes to become. The letter was first printed in 1939 by *V. Helfert* in his *Janáček,
a Study in the Fight for Art and Life.* Vol. I. p. 154.

23. FEELINGS ABOUT BEETHOVEN

When I was 25 years old, I had Beethoven's *Missa Solemnis*
at my fingertips. I conducted it in Brno on the 2nd April, 1879.
But to tell the truth, Beethoven's works left me cold; they never
took me out of myself. They never carried me to a world of ecstasy.
I came to know them too well, too soon. But this was also the reason
why they had such possesion of my soul. In their broad flow I could
feel the power of the firmament, see the sun bathing the clouds in
melody and banishing the shadows; and over all this, the moon pour-
ing out her loneliness. But what of it—I want to be in direct contact with the clouds, I want to feast my eyes on the blue of the sky,
I want to gather the sun's rays into my hands, I want to plunge
myself in shadow, I want to pour out my longings to the full: all
directly.

In the choir of the Leipzig Conservatoire, I was made first
bass, Reinecke was the conductor of Beethoven's *Missa Solemnis*
—it was towards the end of that same year, 1879. But I escaped
from the choir, failed to attend rehearsals, and avoided the performance of the work.

Janáček's reply to an article in the Berlin Magazine *Die Literarische Welt* on the influence
of Beethoven on modern music. The reply was published in translation by the Czech literary
historian *Arne Novák* (1880—1939) in *Lidové Noviny* on 29th March, 1927. — *Beethoven's Missa
Solemnis* was written in the year 1823 and dedicated to his friend and pupil, the Archduke
Rudolph, Archbishop of Olomouc. Janáček gave a performance of it in Brno on the 2nd April,
1879. — *Karl Reinecke* (1824—1910) was a professor at the Leipzig Conservatoire from 1860.
He taught Janáček singing.

24. RESULT OF THE LEIPZIG STUDIES

Mr. Leoš Janáček attended my classes in the theory of music and in piano playing and showed exemplary diligence. His unusual talent for composition, his quick grasp of theoretical principles, his perseverance when doing exercises in counterpoint and the study of fugue, helped him to excellent results. Not least of his successes was in piano playing. His thoroughness in purifying his technique and his subtle sense of phrasing awaken the liveliest hopes for his successful career as a pianist. Finally, it is necessary to stress in what a praiseworthy fashion Mr. Janáček devotes his great interest to musicology. With what enthusiasm he attends the lectures on the history and theory of music at the University.

Dr. Oskar Paul,

> Profesor of Musicology at the Leipzig University and teacher at the Royal Conservatoire of that town.

Leipzig, the 6th December, 1877.

Paul's report is reproduced from Helfert's *Janáček*, vol. I., p. 122. — *Dr Oskar Paul* (1836—1898) was from 1872 professor at the Leipzig University, and from 1869 taught at the Leipzig Conservatoire.

25. JANÁČEK'S FOURTH ROMANCE

On the 27th October, 1877, Professor Paul set him to compose three romances as a study in composition. Janáček worked, however, until the 27th November of that year on more than three romances. He was mainly dissatisfied with these, because he felt, first, that he had been too loose with their form, and secondly, that they failed to suggest the real mood of a romance. Of the romances he wrote, only the fourth has survived. It was begun some time during the morning of the 16th November and was finished that same day in the afternoon. In a letter to his future wife, Miss Zdenka Schulz, he wrote (17th November, 1877) that it would please her, that it contained nice harmonic modulations, but that it had been considered a little too "wuchtig". The magazine *Dalibor* of the 20th November, 1877, published an account of this romance taken from Janáček's letters. Three romances for violin and piano were written as exercises. Professor Paul liked them for their Czech character and arranged for them to be played at a students' concert under the title *Czech Romances*. No record exists to show that either this performance or the perfomance of the fourth romance, in the year 1877, ever took place. The fourth romance, the eightpage original of which I discovered in the Music Library of the State Male Teachers' Training Institute in Brno, was probably played at a number of students' concerts of that Institution. Its existence came to be known only after the death of the composer. The first performance was given from the Brno Broadcasting Station at a concert by Jan Štědroň (violin) and B. Štědroň (piano), which also included Janáček's *Dumka* and *Sonata*. The whereabouts of the other three romances has not yet come to light. The fourth romance is of great importance when studying Janáček's growth as a composer. It is a reflection of his youth and shows how he first began to free himself from his classico-romantic upbringing.

Paul criticised it for being "wuchtig" probably because of its heavy opening section and conclusion. It is clear that the vehement, aggressive Janáček could bring himself only with difficulty to compose in a delicate, gracious mood. However, the romance has a sensitive, passionate melodiousness, bold harmonizations and modulations, and a well-constructed ternary form with similar opening and closing sections.

From my preface for the printed edition of the fourth romance. — *Jan Štědroň*, born 1907, Czech violinist.

26. REPORT FROM THE LEIPZIG CONSERVATOIRE

On the 12th December, 1879, Janáček received his official report rom the Leipzig Conservatoire with the following criticisms:

Theory and Composition: Extraordinarily gifted, a serious and hard-working pupil who shows remarkable progress.

(Oskar Paul.)

Piano playing: A very able, intelligent, and hard-working pupil, who has made very good progress which leads us to expect the most gratifying results from him in the near future.

(E. S. Wenzel.)

An exemplary pupil from all points of view who attains the best results. It is my sincere wish that Janáček should continue with his studies, as his talent and industriousness lead us to expect great things of him.

(Oskar Paul.)

Organ playing: Has proved himself not only to have talent but also diligence. I am very satisfied with him and would like to see him given every possibility of finishing his studies, to which he devotes himself with unusual earnestness, so that he may achieve real excellence in the future.

(Dr Rust.)

Lectures: Attends and shows a lively interest in the subjects.

(Oskar Paul.)

Singing: Attends rarely.

(Karl Reinecke.)

Has a good voice, attended only two or three times at the beginning.

(Klesse.)

Janáček's report from the Leipzig Conservatoire was partly published in German by *V. Helfert* in his *Janáček*, Vol. I. pp. 122. Janáček's teachers at the Conservatoire are given in brackets. The name of *Leo Grill*, from whom Janáček profited most, is missing. — *Oskar Paul* (1836—1898), *Ernst Ferdinand Wenzel* (1808—1880), teacher of piano playing at the Conservatoire. — *Dr. Wilhelm Rust* (1822—1892), excellent German organist, cantor of St. Thomas', Leipzig. He took great trouble in publishing the work of his famous predecessor at St. Thomas', Johann Sebastian Bach. — *Heinrich Klesse* taught choir singing at the Conservatoire.

27. AT THE VIENNA CONSERVATOIRE

Janáček's plan to set out for Vienna after Easter, 1880, took shape as a result of his boundless longing for Zdeňka and is evident from a letter written to her on the 25th January of that year. In it he tells her, how deeply he longs for her and of his feeling of isolation and dissatisfaction with the Conservatoire: "To be nearer to you, to see you more often, to be among people who are less strange to me, not to be always so thrown back on myself, to be hearing new things and having to fight my way in order to gain recognition—that is what I need."

After Easter which he spent in Brno, Janáček went to Vienna to finish his musical studies. On the 1st April he was admitted as a second year student at the Musikfreunde Conservatoire of Music and Dramatic Art. His piano professor was Josef Dachs and for composition he joined the class of Franz Krenn. Janáček found that he could not get on with Dachs, but, not wanting to make a change, he decided to discontinue his piano studies. But with Krenn he was also dissatisfied. He could not bring himself to agree with the neoromantic atmosphere of Krenn's class. Janáček was thus forced into a state of silent rebellion. On the decision of Krenn, Janáček's violin sonata was to have been entered for a competition. However, the commission who heard the work at a rehearsal decided against allowing it to be entered on the grounds that it was too academic. Janáček, however, stood his ground and left the Conservatoire prematurely.

See Helfert's *Janáček*, I. p. 161 ff. — *Josef Dachs*, (1829—1896), teacher of piano playing at the Vienna Conservatoire. — *Franz Krenn* (1816—1897), Professor of Composition in that institution and author of the book *Theoretisch–praktische Musik– und Harmonielehre* (1880).

28. DISAGREEMENT WITH THE COMMITTEE AND THE DIRECTOR

I write to you, but I am unable to find words to describe my feelings, I am in great conflict with my most inner self—on the other hand, I have to laugh. It is so beautifully easy to condemn people. Today I was informed by the commission that, after hearing the Adagio of my Violin Sonata, I am not to be entered for the competition. Krenn told me that they evidently could not warm up to it. I don't blame those gentlemen, not even Beethoven's Adagio would warm me up if I had been listening, for three solid hours, to pupils' compositions. Krenn was sorry that his advice was not taken. As for me, I am left with my conviction that my Sonata is, nevertheless, the best piece which was entered. The works were not looked over by the commission, they were simply played one after another, from three in the afternoon until six o'clock, and then judged. When I was working on my Sonata, I was mainly concerned with constructing a good example of sonata form which would be carried through to a convincing end. The other sonatas had only one movement complete and none of these were in sonata form. I do not mention the word technique, but this made no difference to the commission, for there was not a single expert on composition among them. What next? As a musician who respects himself, I must either write to the Director, assuring him that I can analyse and point out the mistakes of all works which were sent in, or else, dearest Zdenči, I cannot bring myself to continue here under such conditions. To receive a report from such a Director simply makes my blood boil.

Janáček's letter to *Miss Zdeňka Schulz* in Brno, 28th May, 1880. — The competition for the Medal of the Vienna Conservatoire was to have taken place on the 25th June. The most advanced students had to submit their works to a commission drawn from that institution, who announced that the slow movement of Janáček's Violin Sonata was too academic and therefore unsuitable for entry. Janáček's feelings on this occasion are well expressed in his letter to Zdeňka Schulz.

29. JANÁČEK – CONDUCTOR OF CHURCH MUSIC IN BRNO

As always during Holy Week, everyone who visited the King's Monastery in the hours of darkness or during the impressive Good Friday service, was given the opportunity of acquainting himself with the full beauty of church singing. The litany and responses exquisitely harmonized, the choir of well-trained singers, commanding the attention of the listeners with perfect performances of Palestrina's *Improperia* and *Vexilla Regis*. Ceremony and song were here united into a harmonious whole, welling up from one source—the spirit of the Catholic faith. Pavel Křížkovský was not conducting his choir on this occasion, as he had been suddenly transferred to Olomouc. He was replaced by his pupil, Mr. Lev Janáček, a young musician who gives rise to truly great hopes.

From the magazine *St. Cecilia*, Vol. I. 5th May, 1874, published in Prague. — *Palestrina's* "*Improperia*", Our Lord's reproach to the people, forms part of the Good Friday service in Roman churches.

30. CHOIR-MASTER OF THE SVATOPLUK SINGING SOCIETY

We are pleased to announce the appointment of the youthful Mr. Lev Janáček as choir-master of the Craftsmen's Music Society, *Svatopluk*, which will mean a new era in the life of that gathering. This promising musician is the best pupil of Křížkovský, whose post he now holds in the Old Brno Church. Not only there, but also as choir-master of the *Svatopluk* and as a composer, he proves himself to be a worthy apprentice of his master. His remarkable musical accomplishments, his unusual talent for composition of the most serious types, his passionate love of art and his determined diligence, are assurances of the high place he will one day occupy among our best musicians. Already, at his first appearance as conductor of the

Svatopluk society on the 27th April, when he performed works specially arranged for them and inspired them into giving a precise and polished performance, especially of his own purely national compositions (very well worked out arrangements of Serbian folk songs) he drew our attention to himself. And later, to an even greater extent, during the inauguration ceremony of the *Svatopluk* banner, which at last, after many unaccountable prohibitions and difficulties was unfurled, of course, privately, and with the minimum of ceremony, on the 5th July of this year (1873) in the main hall of the Beseda house. Under his baton the choral work, for male voices "To Moravia", by Dr. Norbert Javůrek, rang out with such precision and fervour that we have seldom heard it so magnificently performed. No less appreciated was Janáček's own chorus, "War Song", although the musical form and the words were rather unequal. But let that not frighten Mr. Janáček. We wish with all our hearts that he may be given the fullest opportunity of furthering his musical education to the utmost and of cultivating his talents as a composer. He will surely not disappoint the high hopes which, in all sincerity, we place in him.

Dalibor, Prague, 1873. — Janáček was appointed choir—master of the *Svatopluk* in Brno on the 13th February, 1873, and conducted the choir until September, 1874, when he left for Prague to study at the School of Organists. The report on the inauguration ceremony of the *Svatopluk* banner (5th July, 1873) at which Janáček conducted Javůrek's *To Moravia* and his own *War Song* was published in the Prague musical magazine *Dalibor*, 1st August 1873, p. 255. — Norbert Javůrek, M. D., (1839—1880) collected Moravian folk—songs in his spare time and wrote male-voice choruses, of which *To Moravia* was the most popular. *War Song* is for male voice choir with accompaniment of piano, trumpet, and three trombones. It was completed in June, 1873, and performed, for the first time, by the *Svatopluk* society on the 5th July, 1873.

31. FOR THE SAKE OF ART AND SOCIAL LIFE

To the Committee of the Craftsmen's Music Society Svatopluk in Brno.

Taking into account the unhappy social conditions of Brno in general and of art in particular, I have decided to work with all the greatest possible perseverance, wherever good material and good will can be found, for the carrying on and cultivation of the art of music.

Having chosen Brno for my sphere of activity, I welcome the proposal of your Committee. Therefore, without further delay, for the sake of art and of our social life, I accept your proposal.

I make no conditions.

Yours respectfully,
Lev Janáček.

Helfert's *Janáček*, vol. I., p. 206. — The letter deals with Janáček's engagement as choir-master of the *Svatopluk* after his return from the Prague School of Organists and was written some time during October, 1875. After a year, Janáček resigned from the *Svatopluk* (in October, 1876), because he had accepted the post of choir-master at the Brno Beseda.

32. ESTEEM FOR SMETANA AND DVOŘÁK

As choir-master of the Brno "Beseda", Janáček set about making the works of Dvořák more widely known. The fact that he then became great friends with Dvořák did not lead him to neglect the works of Smetana. Janáček not only realized Smetana's significance in the field of opera, but after taking over at the Brno "Beseda" (1876) introduced the study of three of Smetana's symphonic poems from the cycle, *My Country*. He performed Smetana's *Vltava* (1880—1881) before the composer's death and later continued with *Vyšehrad* (1886) and several choral works, e.g. *Dedication*, the sextet from the *Bartered Bride* and *Peasant's Song* (1884). Janáček devoted the whole of his artistic strength to performing large-scale choral works, for example, Dvořák's *Stabat Mater* (1882) and *The Spectre's Bride* (1888), Mozart's *Requiem* (1878) and Beethoven's *Missa Solemnis* (1879). Dvořák was the only great Czech composer whom Janáček really admired. Janáček changed his opinion of some of Smetana's works after World War I. In 1924 he published an article in the paper, *Lidové Noviny*, in which he shows his full admiration for Smetana's realism, national character and subtlety.

According to Janáček, Smetana wrote powerful works which achieved what they set out to attain. Smetana's works are never gloomy and oppressive. In this way, Janáček showed that it was necessary for each artist to go his own particular way. The sensitive, broad conception of Smetana's work has become national so that, in the words of Janáček, "Smetana's bright personality will remain among us for ever"...

From my article on Smetana and Janáček in *Lidové Noviny* and from Janáček's article about Smetana which appeared in *Lidové Noviny*, 2nd March, 1924.

33. THE CULT OF DVOŘÁK AT THE BRNO BESEDA

It is quite unjust to suppose that I am prejudiced against Smetana. I have not taken the least part in the present conflict. My association with Dvořák is quite accidental. Each of his new works—except his operas—was suitable for concert programmes. Do not regard me as a professional conductor. After all these years of toil, my name has been shamefully exploited. Who has there been, recently, except Smetana and Dvořák? The place of the first is the theatre, where I have no influence; the other belongs to the concert platform. There I did my duty... I have a different opinion of Smetana as a dramatic composer. I am not afraid of holding to my opinion nor of speaking it openly. Malice is unknown to me. I remain Yours respectfully

Leoš Janáček.

Brno, 10th April 1910.

From a letter to *Artuš Rektorys*, first published in the *Correspondence of Leoš Janáček and Artuš Rektorys*, Hudební Matice, Prague, 1949, p. 102. — The conflict, which Janáček refers to, was probably that of 1874—1875, when František Pivoda (1824—1898) made some sharp attacks on Smetana in his paper *Hudební listy*. Janáček published his opinion of Smetana as a dramatic composer in his magazine *Hudební listy* which came out in Brno in 1884—1886, and in the paper *Moravské listy* (1890—1892), of which he was the music critic. — *Artuš Rektorys*, b. 1870, Czech writer on music and editor of Janáček's correspondence.

34. CRITICISM OF A CONCERT CONDUCTED BY JANÁČEK

The Jubilee Concert of the Brno Beseda Music Society, which took place on the 10th January, 1886, was held in the main reception room of the Beseda Hall and was attended by great numbers of Czech intelligentsia from Brno and the surrounding countryside. The programme was arranged with unusual artistic tact and included one of the earlier works of Dvořák, his magnificent *Hymnus*, and the D minor symphony, a perfect example of his maturity as a composer. These works were followed very suitably by Křížkovský's choral work "Utonulá" (The Drowned Woman). As far as the performance of the three works is concerned, the highest praise should go both to the conductor and to the artists taking part. The excellent choir and the conductor's firm control had made of the concert a triumph for the composers. The most subtle nuances and the smallest details of Dvořák's deeply felt work were given their fullest significance. The gradation and phrasing of the choir was inimitable and none of Dvořák's characteristic details were allowed to pass by the orchestra. The public of Brno and its surroundings expressed delight and the utmost enthusiasm during the concert. The magnitude of the performance should have far-reaching results, not only for local music but for Czech music in general.

Kovařovic's review of the Jubilee Concert of the Brno Beseda, conducted by Janáček, which was published in the magazine *Hudební listy*, Vol. II., Brno, 15th January, 1886. — *Karel Kovařovic* (1862—1920) was, at that time, conductor of the Czech National Theatre in Brno (1885—1886). He became famous for the masterly way in which he later handled the post of Opera Director of the National Theatre in Prague (1900—1920) and also for his opera *The Dogheads* based on Alois Jirásek.

35. JANÁČEK AS CONDUCTOR

If you are working scientifically on the work of Leoš Janáček, I would like to take the opportunity of suggesting to you that this would be the moment to speak of Janáček as a conductor, more than has so far been done. He was, in my opinion, a conductor in the full sense of the word and not a mere composer-conductor. Janáček—a true conductor—second only to Karel Kovařovic, has so far not been fully estimated. He was a great artist, who not only knew how to present large - scale works convincingly, both dynamically and rhythmically, but was a conductor who had complete technical understanding of each work, which is surely one of the most important conditions for a successful orchestral ensemble and for the perfect balancing of the wood-wind and brass, etc. During his later years, Janáček's health prevented him from conducting. Once, when I asked him, he replied in his joking way, "I don't conduct because I have a bad heart." I have had you in my thoughts for some time, and today, when I write to you, I feel bound to add my opinion, that Janáček, the conductor, cannot be placed in the same class as the composer-conductors who, in every respect, fail to attain to his conducting ability.

From a letter which *Pavel Dědeček*, Professor of Conducting at the Prague Conservatoire, wrote in reply to my request for some recollections of Janáček. — *Pavel Dědeček* (1885—1954), taught under Janáček at the Brno School of Organists and was conductor of the Brno National Theatre 1908—1914.

36. FOUNDER AND DIRECTOR OF THE BRNO SCHOOL OF ORGANISTS

In the 'seventies of the last century, Janáček began considering the establishment of his own school of organists at Brno, which was also to be an institute of art for the whole of Moravia. After studying at the organ schools of Prague and of other towns abroad, he was convinced of the necessity for a similar type of school in Moravia. In Brno he began by forming a group which undertook to raise the standard of church music in Moravia, and which was to be organized and maintained by the Organ School. In June, 1881, the school was approved, and in December of that year Janáček was appointed Director. The first year was devoted to preparatory work. In the beginning of the year 1882, Janáček worked out the statutes and the school curriculum. In September 1882 the Statute was approved and the Brno School of Organists opened.

—

§ 1. The aim of the Brno School of Organists is to train organists and choir-masters thoroughly in all branches of music both theoretical and practical.

§ 2. The course will be spread over a period of three years. At the end of the first year, the pupil who has diligently applied himself will be able to become organist of a country parish church. During the second year, the pupil should advance sufficiently to be able to take a post as organist of a town parish church. The third year will be devoted to the training of future choir-masters...

From the organisation Statute of the Brno School of Organists. — For futher information on Janáček's work at the Organ School see *Dr Ludvík Kundera's* book *Janáček's School of Organ Playing* (Olomouc, 1948).

37. AGITATES FOR A COLLEGE OF MUSIC

To The Imperial Ministry

in Vienna.

At the time when the taking over of the conservatoire by the state is being discussed, the Association for the Improvement of Sacred Music in Moravia, which is supporting the School of Organists enabling it to provide a three year's course and also a ten month's course for organists of the smaller parishes, humbly puts forward the request that a master-class in organ playing also be instituted for which, however, a state grant would be necessary. It can be stated with certainty, that a sufficient number of musically talented pupils would be available to warrant the establishment of a master-class in organ playing, attached to the Brno School of Organists. The appointed Professor of organ playing should receive a salary sufficient to ensure his being able to devote his entire time to his duties at the school. Concerts should be given daily and the material used during the courses fully controlled, the inclusion of new works being insisted on. The Professor should be entrusted with the entire teaching curriculum of the master-class; that is to say, at least 14 hours a week.

Report of the Director of the Brno School of Organists. — Director's Report — 28th Anniversary Report from the year 1909 proves the modern and progressive way in which Janáček directed the organisation of the Organ School to which he wanted to add a master-class.

38. REFUSES TO COMPOSE A HYMN

I am entirely unable to understand or approve your objections to the Hymn in praise of St. Thomas . . . Such an attitude reflects unfavourably on yourself. You are not only a composer but also the Director of the Organ School and, as such, it is your duty, both to yourself and to that institution, to use your influence in favour of the Hymn-book. The hymn, for which you should write a simple melody, is a good one and admirably suits the purpose for which it is intended. St. Thomas being the student's patron saint, the hymn would become the hymn of student youth.

From a letter written by *Dr Karel Eichler* on the 22nd March, 1910, requesting Janáček, in vain, to set a Latin hymn in praise of St. Thomas. — *Dr Karel Eichler* (1845—1917), biographer of Pavel Křížkovský and editor of a popular hymn-book, *The Way to Everlasting Salvation.*

It was during September of the year 1882 that teaching was first begun at the Brno School of Organists. Nine pupils were accepted as first-year students, subsequently, courses were begun every three years until the year 1905-1906, when all three annual courses began to be taught simultaneously. The school was first housed in a small class–room of the Royal Imperial Czech Teachers' Training Institute of Old Brno. It was soon moved to the winter-garden of the Blue Globe in Old Brno Street. We have occupied the present rooms in No. 1 Jakubská Street from the year 1895-1896, and we are now preparing for removal to our own building.

Change of residence!

God grant that the institute will continue in its original mood of enthusiasm, perseverance and faith in its future. We could scarely have hoped for a better ending to the first twenty-five years, especially the assurance which is given to all graduated, that they may at once become "b r e a d - w i n n e r s". According to the decrees of the Curia of Olomouc and the Bishop's Curia of Brno, a l l a v a i l a b l e p o s t s o f c h o i r - m a s t e r i n t h e w h o l e o f M o r a v i a a r e t o b e r e s e r v e d f o r g r a- d u a t e s o f t h e O r g a n S c h o o l.

P r o c l a m a t i o n !

Our people, who have produced such an admirable amount of folk songs of so rich a variety and of such varying types, deserve to be given all possible means of educating themselves musically, so as to avoid mere haphazard growth or even the neglect and destruction of their culture. The mournful and gay tones of the violin, bagpipes and cymbalom, which were so closely associated with folk song, have fallen silent and with them the songs, both gay and religious. In every village we come across people who are gifted musically, both singers and players who have taught them-

5. Leoš Janáček at the time when he composed *Jenufa* (1901—1902).

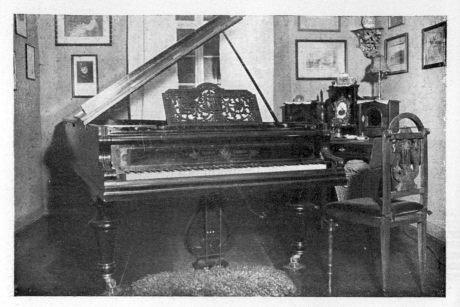

6. Janáček's study in the house close to the Organ School.

selves to play the fiddle, the clarinet, the bugle, etc. Why should not such people, if given the opportunity, be able to learn enough of music and acquire sufficient judgement, to be able to spread and encourage good music among their fellows? Considering this matter to be important, the Council for Raising the Standard of Church Music in Moravia decided to establish a ten-month course attached to the School of Organists in Brno, to educate local organists for their own villages. Normally, it is impossible for a village organist to be a professional musician, on account of the post being so badly paid.

Report of the 25th Anniversary of the Organ School, 1906. — From the Organ School Directors' report for the year 1905—6. Janáček here points out the development of the Organ School which was housed in various buildings and finally, in 1906, was preparing to move into its own building in what is to—day Lenin Street, where it now forms part of the Conservatoire. The report also shows how well Janáček looked after the future of all those who graduated from the school and also how he raised the standard of musical education in out-of-the-way village churches by establishing a ten-month's course for village organists.

40. JANÁČEK THE TEACHER

At the school, Janáček looked after us like a father. He knew all our secrets and from what types of families we came. If one of us got ill, he came at the first opportunity to our rooms to enquire after us. Sometimes it became almost awkward, especially if our illnesses were of a lighter kind and he arrived to find us out! The next day, his anger would burst forth at school and many of us were thus thrown out of the class, usually not for long, however— Janáček's fits of temper quickly cooled. He was the very life and soul of the school. He seemed to be everywhere and knew about all that went on. His harmony lessons were far from pleasant for those who lacked talent and had only "straw" in their heads, as Janáček used to say. Slow thinking irritated him, also prolonged, unadventurous compositions. He liked us to express ourselves in short, concise terms, which was, in fact, his own method of self–expression. A quick judgment of this or that combination, of a mood, of certain musical phrases, etc. His teaching was anything but dull and he never failed to rouse the imagination of every thoughtful and sensitive student. His lessons never became dry lectures, given according to some well tried-out pedagogical system. On the contrary, they gave us glimpses of something from a higher plane of thought which was, for some, hard to understand. It therefore very often happened, that he would abruptly leave the class on discovering that no one was able to keep up with his momentary mood or the flights of his artistic thought. All this sounds very unpedagogical; however, anyone who has comprehended him completely as an artist will fully understand how Janáček roused and inspired one. His lessons in musical form were utter enjoyment. When I compare them with the lessons which I took with Max Reger, I realize that they were far more gripping and inspiring.

From *Jaroslav Kvapil's* article *Leoš Janáček — Director of the Organ School*, which appeared in the musical magazine *Hudební rozhledy*, Vol. I., Brno, 1924-5. — *Jaroslav Kvapil* (1892), Professor of the Janáček Academy of Music and Dramatic Art in Brno, studied under Janáček at the Organ School from 1906 to 1909 and taught there from 1909 to 1911. Kvapil studied with Reger at the Leipzig Conservatoire from 1911 to 1913.

41. FOR TRUTH IN LIFE AND IN ART

I am reminded of one especially enthralling lesson with Leoš Janáček in the year 1907. He was explaining the difference between the old opera overtures and the short introductions to modern operas ... He said, "I have here with me to-day the introduction to my opera *Jenufa* as an example. It has already gone to press, but I was able to bring it and show it to you." With that he began analysing the introduction to the first act. We listened, with bated breath, not only to the music but also to his words and each one of us felt the tremendous originality of the music, music such as we had never heard before. Janáček, the Director, seemed almost to evaporate, leaving before our eyes a great composer creating new music. His last words were: "Jenufa braces herself and sets out to meet life. You are, all of you, young and therefore I impress upon you: Let truth be your guide not only in life, but also in art." With that he left us and the lesson had ended. It was the first of many such lessons and one which I will certainly remember till the end of my life.

By *Vilém Petrželka*, b. in 1889, Professor at the Janáček Academy of Music and Dramatic Art, a pupil of Janáček and Novák. In 1928 he published some Memoirs concerning his teacher in the Brno magazine *Hudební rozhledy*, vol. IV.

42. FOR NEW, ORIGINAL MUSIC

Janáček's teaching activities were twofold: at the Teachers' Institute and at the Organ School. At the Institute he found his work a torture, a trade, necessary to insure his livelihood, which knocked all the artistic buoyancy and spirit out of him. At the school, however, he was in his element, giving it all his love and care and satisfying his inner needs. His lessons were saturated with the ardent passion of his personality and, especially latterly, when teaching the principles of form, he instilled into us his artistic convictions. When discussing his topic, he presented his material logically and precisely, using the most appropriate words and the most concise terms. "Accurate expression shows accuracy of thought", was his slogan. There were sometimes stormy scenes when he refused to allow any circumscribing of the subject, but demanded the only possible description of the matter under consideration. One after another, we got up and we sat down again. Janáček gave us no help, exhorting us to intensive thought. He never ceased to impress upon us that only those compositions which contained something fundamentally new had any sense or value. On the other hand, Janáček was inclined to overlook dexterity in composition. The teaching of harmony and counterpoint was never one of the strong points at the Organ School. Janáček allowed certain students to develop naturally, without either forcing or stunting their growth. The institute, at which there were in the beginning only three teachers (Janáček, Kment, Nesvadba) and at which, even during my student days, only one course was taught each year, at which we were all squeezed together in hired rooms, today flourishes in its own building where, from the year 1908, all three courses have been taught simultaneously by eleven teachers. The intensity of Janáček's endeavours and efforts will be shown, to their full, when history is written.

By *Jan Kunc*, born in 1883, composer and former Director of the Brno State Conservatoire. Studied at the Brno School of Organists from 1901 to 1903. He published the above description of Janáček as a teacher in the Prague musical paper, *Hudební Revue*, vol. IV, 1911 pp. 186-7. — *Jan Kment* (1860—1907), choir-master of the Minorite Monastery in Brno, taught at the Brno School of Organists from 1881 to 1891. — *Jan Nesvadba* (1829—1899), choir-master of the Dome Church of Brno, taught singing at the Brno School of Organists from 1881 to 1888.

43. DEVELOPMENT OF THE ORGAN - SCHOOL

After the first difficult years, when the organ school had nine pupils and three teachers and carried on its work in the unwanted rooms of another institution, it gradually won through and, in 1919, not only had 186 pupils and 13 teachers, but also its own building. With this growth, the school truly became an artistic and scientific institution. Janáček's personality was certainly the main reason for the success of the institute. He insisted on equal care being given to country and town students, but the mere educating of organists would not have given the school its wide importance if Janáček had not made a point of extending the scope of the teaching. Piano playing, violin playing and wind-instrument playing (oboe and clarinet) were also taught there. Each student was given a thorough grounding in musical theory (harmony, rhythm, form), instruction in improvisation and a knowledge of musical history. Also the rudiments of psychology, pedagogy and liturgy, lessons in counter-point and fugue writing and in hymn and choir singing. Janáček even considered establishing a master-class in organ playing, which would have given the Brno school of organists all the main branches necessary for a complete musical education. The future Conservatoire, which Janáček inaugurated in 1919, differed from the school only in that the course was extended from four to seven years and the musical education intensified. From all this we see how easily the Organ School became the Conservatoire, expecially if we consider the analytical discussions which concluded the sonata-evenings, the lectures, concerts and productions, which the school sponsored; and then the teaching staff, who were all taken over into the organization of the Conservatoire; in short, a perfect forebear for the Brno Conservatoire.

From my article written for the 25th Anniversary of the Brno Conservatoire, which appeared in the musical magazine *Smetana*, vol. XXXVII, 1940, p. 140.

44. PSYCHOLOGICAL EFFECT OF HARMONIC PROGRESSIONS

Play quietly the incomplete dominant chord of C (G—B—F) with the right hand; with the left strike loudly the tonic chord of A flat (A flat—C—E flat) leaving the dominant chord of C held. The resulting sound is chaos. The clashing colours of this effect result from the feelings aroused by the tones of the first chord being combined with the false feelings of the second. — But let us now bring order to this chaotic moment. First, the notes of the right hand gradually die away; second, similarly the A flat chord softens, although not so soon in so far as it was later struck; third, we are left with only the A flat chord sounding. Let us now repeat the process artificially. We hear more clearly a very impressive and arresting echo, emanating from the sounding chaos. Raise the fingers one after another, beginning with the highest note (F), and ending with the lowest, slowly, finger after finger. What a pleasant emotion now grips us while we are being led to a full comprehension of the sounding chaos! This is not surprising: the harmonic combination arising from A flat and F, that is to say, the feelings and false feelings aroused by the tones of this sixth finally die away, and we are left with the consonant fifth sounding clearly. Similarly, the harmonic combination of the notes of the second chord, when combined with those of the first, becomes more pleasant. After the storm, peace; after the grey clouds, the sun breaks through — that is the exact effect.

In this way, we could enumerate the harmonic combinations which are agitating in effect, calming in effect, etc. This is the source from which our deepest musical feeling springs and which is capable of reaching the highest points and the most subtle nuances. This is the source of truth which must be apparent to all who possess a healthy sense of hearing whether they be laymen or artists.

From the introduction to Janáček's book *The Harmonic Combination of Chords* (Prague, 1897) which was later extended and became his textbook *The Complete Book of Harmony*, Brno, 1920. — Janáček constructed his theory from a psychological point of view and based it on the work of Max Wundt (1832—1920) and Herman L. F. Helmholtz (1821—1894) and his book *Die Lehre von den Tonempfindungen*) 1863.

45. JANÁČEK REJECTS KOVAŘOVIC'S OPERA

The theatre bill of the 8th January 1887 read as follows:

> An   original   novelty !
> First   performance
> The   Bridegrooms

Comic opera etc. set to music by K a r e l   K o v a ř o v i c — (At the National Theatre, well and succesfully performed.)

Which t u n e did you remember? Or at least which t h e m e? In what sense is this opera dramatic? I would not have written "set to music by" but "s t a g e d s i m u l t a n e o u s l y w i t h m u s i c", Macháček's comedy, etc. Libretto and music are quite independent. Write a new opera to the libretto and some sort of drama to that so-called music, filled with menacing obscurity, desperate screams and dagger stabs. Therefore that unusual phenomenon: it was Macháček's and not Kovařovic's *Bridegrooms* who succeeded once or twice in making us laugh. The overture, with its uncertain harmony and wavering sense of key, gives proof of the musical talent: to induce considerable deafness.

Janáček's sharp criticism of Kovařovic's opera, *The Bridegrooms*, which was performed at the Brno National Theatre on the 8th January, 1887 every word of which was published, shows how Janáček struck at Kovařovic's novelty in the Brno magazine, *Hudební listy*, Vol. III of 15th January, 1887. This type of criticism certainly influenced Kovařovic in his later unfavourable attitude to Janáček's *Jenufa* when, from 1900, Kovařovic was Director of the Opera at the Prague National Theatre. — *Karel Simeon Macháček* (1799—1846), Czech playwright.

46. JANÁČEK ON SMETANA'S *DALIBOR*

We observe with pleasure the appearance of this almost completely discarded opera. Also, we were given excellent time to prepare ourselves for this rare occasion: the first performance in Brno on the 16th January of Smetana's *Dalibor*. The effect was powerful, universal—almost dazzling. However, we are gradually recovering from our enchantment and, for the second performance, it will not be amiss to consider, separately, the individual sections.

After the waves of a storm have receded, the first things to appear are little islands of most delightful melody in well thought-out form and completely Czech style. The main part, Dalibor, is rich in such moments of which we would cite, for example, his first aria "I ever resisted woman's charm..."; his beautiful duet with Milada: "What is life to me? I care not if I die today or live on till tomorrow..." with its effective change from G major to G minor and back. Less effective is his entrance at the words: "Have you heard it, my friend, as it sounds from heaven?" Here the modulations from D flat to D and from E flat through E to D flat are a trifle conventional. Most effective, owing to their excellently worked-out form, are the duet in the second act (Jitka and Vítek: "Oh, what longing brings us to each other...!") which recommends itself by the continuous sounding of the note F; the aria of the jailor, Beneš: "How sad the jailor's life...!" and Dalibor's aria (in prison): "Oh, Zdeněk, if only God would grant...!" impress us especially by their perfection of form.

From Janáček's criticism of Smetana's *Dalibor* produced at the Brno National Theatre on the 16th January, 1888. One of many documents showing Janáček's aesthetic formalism which was his conscious guide when making criticism.

47. PROPAGATOR OF DVOŘÁK'S WORKS

Janáček, thirteen years younger than Dvořák, worshipped the great composer and took him for his example. To Dvořák, he submitted his first opera *Šárka* (1887) for criticism and probably also *Amarus* (1897) as he had already dedicated his male-voice choruses to Dvořák "in token of unbounded respect".

From their first meeting in the early 'seventies, Janáček was so much attracted to Dvořák, that a strong and lasting friendship began to develop between them. This is proved not only by their friendly relations and frequent visits, but also by their correspondence starting in 1880, and their journeying together in the summer of 1883 from Vysoká to Prachatice through Husinec, Strakonice, Orlík, Písek, Karlův Týn, stopping at the Říp and at Dvořák's birthplace, Nelahozeves near Kralupy. Besides, it is a known fact that Janáček occupied Dvořák's rooms at No. 10 Žitná Street, during 1883 while Dvořák was on his summer holidays.

From this it is clear that Janáček was steeped in the music of Dvořák. His frequent performances of Dvořák's work in the Brno Beseda was responsible for their being spread throughout the whole of Moravia. He encouraged their performance at the Teacher's Training Institute, and after Dvořák's death, arranged a Dvořák evening at the Friends of Art Club in Brno (1906); he used every opportunity of spreading enthusiasm when writing criticism, analysis and articles. It is therefore not strange that his earlier works show a strong Dvořák influence. Indeed, he called the scores of Dvořák's masterpieces, his chief aids. Dvořák was never satisfied with merely clear, interesting harmonic progressions with a single melody; he builds up simultaneously two, three or even five expressive themes. Dvořák's scores easily become dear to a musician's heart. Janáček makes an interesting condemnation of the barrenness of Wagner's introduction to *Tristan and Isolde* compared to Dvořák's dramatic construction in *The Spectre's Bride*. Janáček was enraptured by the adagio of Dvořák's G major Quartet (op. 106) and admired Dvořák's ability to present the same musical thought in so many different ways. Proof of this may be found in his note-books. He mentions Dvořák's *Legends* as most beautiful and most dramatic, and calls his *Poetic Tone-Pictures* for piano, op. 85, enchanting and faithfully worked-out little compositions. He gives his reminiscences of Dvořák in the introduction to the symphonic poem *The Water-goblin*, where he makes the following interesting judgement: "We could bring forward innumerable documents to prove that the most characteristic of Dvořák's compositions are strongly expressive and dramatic." He was always one of those who felt the strong dramatic feeling which penetrates Dvořák's works.

Janáček, to the end of his life, remained Dvořák's most staunch supporter. Especially noteworthy is his condemnation of the so-called fight for Dvořák, which occurred at the begining of World War I. He condemned the attacks which accused Dvořák of lacking originality in the following words: "We have long passed the stage of ferreting out 'borrowed' themes. Unfortunately, here it is still the fashion. It is futile, disagreeable and utterly senseless. They aim at denying Dvořák's originality. They forget that originality cannot be judged superficially. It is absurd to consider the themes separately, without considering the compositions as a whole."

Again he writes: "The Czechs of Brno will have much to understand before they can appreciate Dvořák, because no one has yet succeeded in comprehending the vastness of his music."

See in detail my essay on Dvořák and Janáček, which appeared in the magazine *Vlastivědný věstník moravský*, Vol. VI, 1951. The four male–voice choruses were dedicated by Janáček to Dvořák *"in token of his most unbounded respect"*.

48. DVOŘÁK ON JANÁČEK'S CHORAL WORKS

Dear Friend,

I received your choral works and send you my thanks, not only for them, but also for the dedication of which I am very proud and which gives me great pleasure. As soon as I had opened the parcel, I read them through several times and I must admit that in many places, especially with regard to your modulations, I was taken aback and unable to form an opinion. I did not go straight away to the piano, I did not play them; I think I understand a thing better, from a theoretical point of view, by merely reading it. But when I had played them through once, twice, three times, my ear gradually became accustomed and I said to myself: well, after all, it may be possible, but we still might argue about it.

That is, however, unimportant. I think they are a real enrichment of our poor literature (poor in that kind of work). They are original, and what is most important they breathe forth a truly Slavonic atmosphere. They are certainly not "Liedertafel". In places, the effect will be enchanting and I hope it will soon be possible to hear them. I congratulate you on your small but at the same time significant composition and hope that you will write many of the kind.

Do not think that I praise you because you have dedicated the work to me. I wanted to tell you at once, but I was afraid to do so. I thought it better to keep my opinion to myself or to tell you later, or to write to you. That is why I read yesterday's article by Novotný in the "Hlas národa" with the utmost pleasure. It is just as I would have written it myself and I am glad that I was not disappointed.

Once more my most sincere thanks for such a precious gift and I remain yours ever

Antonín Dvořák.

Vysoká, 13th September, 1886.

Dvořák's letter to Janáček was printed in an article by *A. Rektorys* entitled *Antonín Dvořák's Letters to Leoš Janáček* (*České Slovo*, 7th February 1933). The same letter was also included in Helfert's *Janáček*, Vol. I. page 361, and also in Otakar Šourek's *Dvořák's Letters to his Czech friends*. (Prague, 1941, page 98—99). — *Václav Juda Novotný* (1849—1922), Czech music critic and translator. His criticism of Janáček's four male—voice choruses appeared in the paper *Hlas národa*, 11th September, 1886.

47. UNDER THE INFLUENCE OF DVOŘÁK

Janáček's lyrical moments always contain a tragic strain. Unlike Smetana, he was unable to write in a purely light-hearted mood. From the technical point of view, Janáček makes the classics his example. The orchestration of the first two acts of *Šárka* has something of Dvořák's sonority but lacks Dvořák's profundity and clarity. It is an opera of great interest in so far as it shows how Janáček's musical individuality was, in the beginning, firmly joined to that of Dvořák. However, Dvořák meant to Janáček something far more than a mere musical example. Janáček literally lived himself into Dvořák's style in order to be able to carry it on logically and to evolve a style of his own.

From *V. Helfert's Janáček.*

50. JANÁČEK ON DVOŘÁK'S ORCHESTRATION

I am convinced that Mr. Dvořák's scores are masterly studies in counterpoint. He is not satisfied with the mere harmonization of a single melody in a clear and interesting way; he combines two, three or even five varying themes. I could compare his scores to a good picture: a single idea recurring in many groups of scattered figures, each face bearing its own particular characteristics. Similarly, the pages of Dvořák's scores are filled with interesting figures which unite to produce a great harmonic thought, without, however, a single one resembling another. A musician grows attached to Dvořák's scores. What is most important, Dvořák never leaves his figures perpetually in one voice; hardly has one of them claimed our interest, than another rises up for notice. We are kept in constant exicitement.

From Janáček's article, *A Few Words on Counterpoint*, which appeared in the Brno Magazine, *Hudební Listy*, Vol. IV, 1st January, 1888, p. 33.

51. HIS FIRST OPERAS (*ŠÁRKA*, AND *THE BEGINNING OF A ROMANCE*)

Janáček's first operas, *Šárka* and *The Beginning of a Romance*, occupy an important place in his development in the handling of opera technique and style. They prove that, from the beginning, he neither denied nor wanted to destroy tradition. On the contrary, both these early works are decidedly traditional in style and only occasionally reach new principles and values which merely go beyond and extend tradition. The tremendous development which took place in Janáček's works during the years 1887—1903 was doomed to remain concealed from and misunderstood by his contemporaries. *Šárka* was first performed after 38 years, and *The Beginning of a Romance*, although given in Brno (10th February, 1894) was abruptly refused by the management of the National Theatre in Prague, who would have nothing to do with it until the year 1916. His ballet, *Rákoš Rákoszy*, however, was performed in Prague (24th July, 1891) during the Jubilee celebrations. In this way, the general public were not given sufficient opportunity of judging the full output of Janáček's manifold art. They considered him to be an authority on folk art, a collector and arranger of folk songs and, as far as composition and theory were concerned, an eccentric innovator.

From the analysis of *Jenufa* (Brno, 1938) by *Dr František Pala* (1887), Czech music critic and author of studies on Janáček's works.

52. THE POET ZEYER REFUSES PERMISSION TO USE HIS *ŠÁRKA* AS A LIBRETTO

Dear Sir,

I am sorry if I cause you any distress but, believe me, I have very serious reasons why I cannot allow you to compose music to my *Šárka*. Actually, you are yourself rather to blame in this affair. Allow me to remind you that it might have been wiser to have asked my premission before planning your opera and sending it out into the world. No doubt you will find another use for your music, so that your time will not have been lost.

In any case my name would do you little good with the management of the National Theatre as I have only ill-wishers there. Forgive me if I have caused you any unpleasantness and remember that you have done the same to me.

Yours very respectfully,

Julius Zeyer.

Vodňany, 10th November 1887.

It was a misunderstanding. I did not know if I would be able to make anything of my first opera, which was the reason why

61

I wrote it for myself without announcing it to anyone. I sent the complete piano score to Dr Dvořák for his opinion. It turned out well, and only after this favourable criticism did I ask Mr. Zeyer for his permission. My work was not sent out into the world as Zeyer supposed.

Leoš Janáček.

Julius Zeyer (1841—1901), Czech poet and novelist, was disappointed by the failure of his works in the National Theatre and refused Janáček permission to use his *Šárka* as an opera libretto. Janáček added a few explanatory lines to Zeyer's letter which appeared in *Max Brod's Leoš Janáček*.

53. *ŠÁRKA* PERFORMED AFTER 38 YEARS

Dear Friend,

Many thanks for the excellent way in which you produced my opera, *Šárka*. I particularly commend your conception of the humiliated women in Act III. That is just how it should be. Another thing is the scene in the vault with the dead Libuše; please would you see to the following alterations:

1. The vault should be in semi—darkness
2. Libuše should be dressed in a white robe. In Slovakia it is still the colour of mourning (Javorník).
3. The crown on her head should shine.
4. Ctirad should not go at once into the vault, but only when he is hidden from view.

On Sunday, Universal Edition's representative is coming to the performance to arrange for the publishing. I hope he will like it. Naturally, after your idea of humiliating the women in Act III, I will ask for you as a producer, if another theatre should be interested in putting on my *Šárka*.

With kindest regards
Yours sincerely,
Leoš Janáček.

To Ota Zítek from Brno, 13th November, 1925.

Please let me have the few words Přemysl is to sing in "Šárka".
The music carried me away and I found myself without any words.

Kindest regards,

Leoš Janáček.

To Ota Zítek from Hukvaldy, 6th November, I925.

Janáček's first opera *Šárka* with libretto by Julius Zeyer, was first performed in its final version with orchestration by Janáček's pupil, *Osvald Chlubna* (1893–) at the Brno National Theatre, 38 years after its completion. The story of the women's revolt, led by Šárka, against the men (Czech mythology) has been set to music by various composers the best known example being Smetana's symphonic poem. *Zdeněk Fibich* (1850–1900) also wrote an opera, *Šárka.—Ota Zítek*, Czech Composer and manager of the Brno National Theatre. He directed the first performances of Janáček's *Šárka, The Excursion of Mr. Brouček, Fox Sharpears* and *The House of the Dead.*

54. *THE BEGINNING OF A ROMANCE* PERFORMED

I welcome tonight's performance of Janáček's opera, *The Beginning of a Romance,* as the first Czech work of worth to be given its première in our theatre. At last the management of our theatre has shown itself worthy of its great artistic mission in Moravia. I also welcome this performance for its entirely Moravian origin, not only the libretto but also the music being our own. Here we are made aware of Czech art as it appears in Moravia. Moravia is not sufficiently rich artistically to be able to allow to-night's performance to go unnoticed in the Czech musical world. We received a gift such as we have never before received: the first truly Moravian opera, a younger sister of the already famous Czech opera.

The author of these lines, *Josef Merhaut* (1863—1917), welcomed with great enthusiasm Janáček's opera, *The Beginning of a Romance,* on the day of the first performance in Brno, 10th February, 1894, in the paper, *Moravská Orlice.*

55. *THE BEGINNING OF A ROMANCE* REFUSED IN PRAGUE

Believe me, the treatment you receive from the management of the National Theatre in Prague would infuriate and pain me far more if I were not only too familiar with the local conditions. Here is something to console you: Bendl was engaged to write an opera, *Son of Tábor*, two and a half years ago; in fact it was written even longer ago. A work by a Czech composer can wait. If Mascagni writes something, they make haste to send him a telegram in order to have it as soon as possible. If they do not decide to put on your work during March, it would be better to leave it until the autumn season, especially as they will keep you waiting anyway until then. Dvořák fared no better, as his librettist, Mrs Červinka, once told me. I refrain from mentioning my own experiences. What can we do about it? You have the consciousness of honest endeavour, the guiding light of talent. Believe me, however many difficulties and obstructions may be thrown in your path, nothing can alter the complimentary way in which everyone is talking about you; praising your great talent and expressing high hopes for your future. I understand the reluctance of one as proud as yourself to go on begging those people. But, may be, your *Beginning of a Romance* would need just that.

However, perseverence will prevail.

Gabriela Preiss.

Janáček did not live to hear the first performance of *The Beginning of Romance* at the National Theatre. — *Gabriela Preiss* (1862—1946) whose story, *The Beginning of a Romance*, was put into verse and made suitable for use as a libretto by Professor *František Rypáček* (1853—1917) pseudonym, *Jaroslav Tichý*. — Her letter, published in part without date by Professor *Pavel Váša* (1874—1954), in an article on Janáček's difficulties with his librettists, in the programme of *D 41* No 4 pp. 123—125, explains the conditions at the National Theatre. — *Karel Bendl* (1838—1897), Czech composer, best known for his choral works and songs. His opera *Son of Tábor*, composed in 1888, was first performed in 1892. — *Marie Červinka-Rieger* (1854—1895), wrote the librettos for two of Dvořák's operas — *Dimitrij* and *The Jacobin*.

7. Leoš Janáček in the Russian Circle in Brno, of which he was founder and Chairman (1897—1915).

8. The Czech National Theatre in Brno, where *Jenufa* was performed for the first time (January 21st, 1904).

56. RECOGNITION BY THE CZECH ACADEMY IN PRAGUE

Dear Sir,

I am very pleased to know that you have found in my poem, *Amarus*, something suitable for being set to music. I am convinced that you will be entirely able to work it out successfully without the interference of a third person.

I have pleasure in informing you that at the meeting of the Czech Academy, which took place on the 1st June, you were awarded, on the recommendation of Mr. Fibich and Mr. Chvála, a subsidy of 200 florins for your work. Although I am not a musician, I did all in my power to bring the affair to a successful conclusion. They were unaware of your letter which I myself received only two days later.

Yours respectfully,

Jaroslav Vrchlický.

Prague, 8th June, 1897.

Letter written by one of the greatest Czech poets, *Jaroslav Vrchlický* (1853—1912). Apart from the cantatas *Amarus* and *Everlasting Gospel*, Janáček also set Vrchlický's *Song of Autumn* for mixed choir. — *Zdeněk Fibich* (1850—1900), creator of the modern scenic melodrama. — *Emanuel Chvála* (1851—1924), Czech composer and music critic who later was one of the first to realise the full significance of Janáček's *Jenufa*.

57. *AMARUS*—THE CANTATA OF COMPASSION

Dear Sirs,

Do not try to make anything unusual out of *Amarus*. Do not try to see in it more than the ordinary words which the poet has written and which I have answered in music. Understand the words and feel the magic of spring and of love — and the work has fulfilled its purpose. Every analysis of the themes makes the comprehension of the work more difficult. Each one of us will imagine his own setting for the story. I imagine the Queen's Cloister in Brno. The long, cool corridors, the silence and the golden sun shining into the shady garden loud with bird-song, the high arches of the church and the almost invisible picture of the Madonna. Close by hangs the silver "eternal light" and Amarus's silent tread disturbs the mute twilight. My youth is in the work. How could it have been otherwise?

First I took it to Ferdinand Vach at Kroměříž. Witnesses are still living who heard how wretchedly it turned out. Let us hope you will fare better.

Yours respectfully,

Leoš Janáček.

Brno, 2nd June 1928.

To the Moravian Singing Club of Kroměříž, which was the first to perform Janáček's lyrical cantata, *Amarus* (2nd December, 1900). Although the performance was conducted by Janáček, the rehearsals were taken by the Moravian choir-master, *Ferdinand Vach*, founder of the Moravian Teacher's choir. The indisposition of the soloists and the insufficiency of numbers in the Kroměříž town orchestra were responsible for the low standard of the performance. The unusual key of A flat minor caused the musicians so much trouble that Janáček, on the advice of Vach, transposed the work from A flat minor to A minor, without sharps or flats. In the year 1928 this cantata was again given by the Kroměříž Moravians, conducted by Eugen Třasoň, to whom Janáček wrote the above letter.

58. JANÁČEK AS A LYRIC WRITER

He lived from tender childhood
within the monastery's walls
Whence came he there he knew not
but being born in sin, they called him Amarus . . .

The beginning of Jaroslav Vrchlický's beautiful poem must have attracted Janáček, who certainly read into it his own childhood at the Queen's Monastery Foundation of Old Brno. The hard life strongly influenced the character of his work. The simplicity of the musical colour suggests the atmosphere of the cloister which is increased by an undercurrent of deep feeling. In my opinion the lines: "There sat the happy ones..." and "In the grave-yard he lay on the tomb of his mother..." may be said to reach the height of lyrical perfection. It is also one of the first indications of Janáček's deviation from Dvořák in his search for new ways of lyrical expression. The alternating of choir and soloist shows the example of the Eastern Church, which Janáček has succeeded in combining with his own fervent, acrid style and dramatic accentuation. Janáček, the natural dramatist, comes into his own in such moments as when Amarus recalls his mother whom he fails to recognize. Here Janáček wields, with heartrending strength, the tones of his favorite A flat minor; without, however, destroying the essentially lyrical character of Amarus.

From my programme of a concert given by the Brno Beseda (1838). — Jaroslav Vrchlický included *Amarus* in the anthology of his works of the years 1875—1892. — Janáček made some very slight alterations to the poem.

59 BORN AND BROUGHT UP AMONG FOLK SONGS AND DANCES

Janáček's creative period from the year 1888 to the year 1905, that is to say from the completion of his opera *Šárka* (1887) to the composing of his operas *Jenufa* and *Fate* (1904), is the period during which he was most intensively interested in folk music, especially the folk songs and dances of Moravia. This period, amounting to almost twenty years, makes up an unusual and independent part of his creativeness, which could be called his classical period in folk style. Naturally, he had long been familiar with folk poetry and folk songs. He had been brought up on Sušil and Bartoš, and very early in his work as a composer had showed a propensity to write in folk style. This was apparent even after *Jenufa*. Folk music guided him during his whole life, more especially as he came from an old and humble family firmly rooted among the peasantry. But the years 1888 to 1905 are his most productive and most dedicated to folk music. All his work as a collector, organiser, lecturer, theoretician, writer, teacher, composer and even conductor, aimed at bringing folk songs and dances and the melodious intonation of folk dialect into its own. If Janáček had not known Moravian folk dances and songs so well, he would never have become so great a genius of Moravian music. The period of awakened interest in folk music in general marks the beginning of Janáček's individual style. He was unusually influenced by folk songs and dances, which he regarded as an infallible source of inspiration. In the melody of speech, that is to say in expressive melodic curves and contours of speech, he saw an even stronger expression of the human spirit.

A few facts and dates throw light on this great period of Janáček's creativeness: after the male-voice choruses (1885) dedicated to Dvořák, and the completion of the opera Šárka, he began, independently, experimenting with Moravian folk songs and dances during his summer holidays of the year 1888 at his birthplace, Hukvaldy, and in Wallachia. In 1889, he wrote a short essay on the different types of Moravian folk songs and dances which was included in Bartoš's revised edition of his National Songs of Moravia. The same year, Janáček also conducted in Brno some of his Wallachian dances for orchestra. In 1890, he published two of these dances Starodávný and Pilky, as op. 2 and began his collaboration with Bartoš on their publication which appeared under the title A Bouquet of Moravian National Songs. At that time Janáček published, in collaboration with a group of ethnographists, three volumes of Moravian National Dances (1891–1893)

On the 24th July, 1891, Janáček's Moravian folk ballet, Rákoš Rákoczy, was given its first performance at the National Theatre in Prague during the Jubilee celebrations. In that year, he also completed his orchestral suite, Op. 3, which included two Wallachian dances. In 1892, he organized a concert of the Velká peasant band, and compiled the first volume of piano accompaniments to Moravian folk songs. In 1894, he conducted his one act folk-opera

The Beginning of a Romance, which he had completed in 1891, in Brno. Also in 1894, he was busy helping with the work of preparing the Ethnographical Exhibition in Prague. He had been invited to Prague to organize the section dealing with Moravian music. In connection with this work he organized and induced people to take part in local exhibitions and competitions, and did all in his power to stir up interest in the exhibition so as to assure the best possible representation for Moravia. From 1899 to 1901 he threw himself into the work of preparing Bartoš's last collection of Moravian folk songs for which he wrote a vast musicological introduction. In 1905 he was made President of the Working Council for Czech National Songs in Moravia and Silesia where he laid the foundations of what is today the Institute for the Promotion of Folk Art in Brno, a branch of the Czechoslovak Academy. Janáček's detailed essay, "Collecting Czech National Songs in Moravia and Silesia" (published in the magazine "Dalibor", 1906), lays out a plan for the collector of folk songs and formally concludes the most productive period of his work in that field. His studies in folk song were significant in that they added great strength and depth to his compositions.

From my introduction to *National Dances of Moravia* (Prague, 1953) — *František Sušil* (1804—1868), editor of Moravian folk songs (1835—1840). — *František Bartoš* published, with Janáček, a new large collection of Moravian folk songs (Prague, 1901, Czech Academy).

60. HIS DANCE STYLE

In Janáček's *Wallachian Dances* everything ferments and thunders. The score is brimming over with vitality. We have no doubt that we possess in Janáček a gifted composer who, in time, will ripen and be understood and valued according to his worth.

From a review of Janáček's *Wallachian Dances* which were performed at a gala performance in aid of the Brno National Theatre in December, 1889 (*Moravské Listy*, Vol. II, 1889, No. 30). He composed them between 1889 and 1890 and published them in the year of their completion. In the second edition, which was brought out by the Prague Hudební Matice in 1928, they were renamed *Lachian Dances*.

61. DMITRI KABALEVSKY ON THE *LACHIAN DANCES*

The two symphonic suites in folk dance style, *Moravian Dances* and *Lachian Dances*, create a great and lasting impression, not only for their gay peasant costumes but also for the high technical standard of the dancers. The greatest success, however, goes to Janáček's music. Both suites are based on folk dance melodies. Both are, however, equally far from every kind of primitive folk art treatment or subjective effervescing or disfiguring of folk art. In them Janáček shows his great gifts and his mastery. The suites are fresh in melodic material, in symphonic construction and orchestral colour. They contain music which is deeply popular, national, and realistic in every way. This, in my opinion is what makes Janáček a truly progressive composer and what links him up with the best traditions in Czech music. In this phase of his work, Janáček certainly leans towards Czech classical music.

From an article by Dmitri Kabalevsky (1904—) published in the magazine *Music of the Soviet Union*, Vol 1, 1950, under the title, *Moravian Dances produced at the National Theatre in Prague 1949*. A set of dance scenes to Janáček's Lachian, Wallachian and Hanakian dances.

62. COLLABORATION WITH FRANTIŠEK BARTOŠ

The proof that folk songs originated from words lies in the special character of their rhythm. There is no possibility of dividing them into bar-lines. The rhythm of folk songs, unbelievably rich in variety, can be put into order only by the words. It is impossible to compose a melody and then add words. In Moravian folk songs, the unusual rhythm makes this especially impossible. Each beat in our songs is reasonable and convincing. Each rhythm is timed and accentuated and the whole song sublimated even from the metric point of view. In every note of each song there is, as I see it, a fragment of an idea. If you leave out a single note from the melody, you perceive that it has become incomplete and has ceased to make sense. In our songs, there is not a single unnecessary note; we say that the note is melodically sure. Folk songs, when combined with physical movement, become dancing songs. Because the limits of the folk songs and folk speech alter, we follow the song with our speech and we follow our speech with the song. To speak imperfectly is to sing imperfectly. The importance of the song, from the point of view of purity of language, is naturaly self-expressive . . .

Folk songs are as beautiful as the language from which they spring and are dependent on the locality in which they are sung, on the time at which they are sung, on the occasion, and mood in which they are sung. These various circumstances change the melody and rhythm of the songs. Among the people, there are no singers who would use the songs on occasions when they are not apt; that is to say, in sympathy with the human heart and the human spirit. For this reason, many songs are sung only very rarely. But fortunately, among the people, there are a great number of singers who preserve the songs in their memories. They are much in demand. They sing in the fields, and at weddings. In their songs, they move the hearts of lovers, and divine and express the longings of young girls. A trio of well-known peasant singers sang for me 600 verses o 58 songs in two evenings. It seemed as though one song prepared the way for the next. If the atmosphere can be enchanted by the perfume of lime-trees and wild thyme, these evenings were surely enchanted by the songs. The singers told me that they knew many more songs.

What a splendid sonority and variety of colour when the fiddles, bagpipes and cymbalom play together. Today, the doublebass plays the lower notes, and instead of bagpipes, clarinets are often used. The melody gains brilliance and strength when these combined instruments break out into sound. These instruments have given our songs rich variety of modulation. . .

The Moravian folk song is characterised by a striking predilection for the seventh degree of the scale. It seems to me as though the melody was purposely descending from the tonic by a whole tone and leaning towards a lower key which contains an emotional impression strong enough to lead the melody into a new key.

This special Moravian inclination to the seventh degree or to the key of the seventh degree in the middle of the song, should be of interest to Czech composers in Bohemia, who show a tendency to use the commonplace inclination to the dominant or the key of the dominant.

The Moravian inclination to the seventh degree of the scale has given to our folk song a special melodic sense. Let us examine, the following song for example

At the beginning of the song the note A is the tonic of A major In the 4th bar it has already modulated to E, after which it descends by measured steps to D which is the tonic of D major.

From Janáček's essay, *Moravian Folk Songs from the Musical Point of View*, which was published in the collection of Moravian folk songs (Prague, 1901, Czech Academy) edited by *František Bartoš*.

63. FOLK SONGS BRING NATIONS TOGETHER

I lived among folk songs from childhood. Each folk song contains an entire man; his body, his soul, his surroundings, everything, everything. He who grows up among folk songs, grows into a complete man. Folk songs are made in a single spirit, which gives men the culture of God and not an injected culture. That is why our music, so long as it springs from this source, will join us in solidarity. Folk songs bind the nation, bind all nations and all people with one spirit, one happiness, one paradise.

From Janáček's speech after a concert of the Mansfield Road, Gospel Oak L. C. C. School Choir in London, which performed his *National Songs of England*. The speech was reported by *Jan Mikota* in an article published in the magazine, *Hudební listy*, Prague, Vol. V, 1925–1927, p. 257.

64. STUDIES IN THE HARMONIZATION OF FOLK MUSIC

To the governing body of the Emperor Franz Josef's Czech Academy of Science, Literature and Art.

The undersigned respectfully takes the liberty of requesting a travelling allowance for the purpose of collecting folk material in Moravia, Hungarian Slovakia and Silesia, so as to be able to know, at first hand, the harmonic aspect of Czech folk music and also to complete our collections of Moravian folk dances. Last year, I took the liberty of putting a similar request to the governing body, too late, however, for the request to be attended to.

To my present request I take the liberty of calling to witness my new series of Czech dances for orchestra and of drawing your attention to my article on the musical lay-out of folk dances of Moravia (*Český lid*, Vol. II. No 4 1893) where, as introduction, I have described the journeys which I have so far undertaken.

There can be no doubt of the importance of getting to know, at first hand, the harmonic aspect of folk music. For example, the taking down of cymbalom playing or the playing of groups of peasant players in Moravian Slovakia during the actual singing and dancing. It is long and difficult work but very urgent, as both the cymbalom players and the players in the peasant bands are dying out.

As my humble means will not allow me to devote enough time to the work and are insufficient to cover the cost of travelling to places of importance for such work, I address the Czech Academy in all hope and belief in their assistance.

In the event of my request being granted, I should be able to collect a wealth of harmonic material in Velká, in Strážnice and its surroundings, and in the southern part of Moravian Silesia. This year I should be able to devote two or even four months of my time to this work.

Yours respectfully,

Leoš Janáček,
Royal Imperial Teacher of Music, and Director
of the Brno School of Organists.

Janáček's request for financial assistance, dated the end of March 1893. — The request was not granted and he was obliged to carry out his work at his own expense.

65. TRAVELS IN SEARCH OF FOLK SONGS

On his travels in search of folk songs, Janáček explored new country. He kept as far as possible from railway communications so as to find folk art in its most unspoiled state. He hired a driver and a farm cart, drawn by an old, under-fed cob. He would have lost too much time if he had gone on foot. As it was, his driver gave him enough trouble. At every hill he had to jump down and help to pull the cart. When going down hill he preferred to walk so as to be sure of reaching the valley without accident. To be sure, the society of Luhačovice Spa is entirely unaware of all this when they meet him walking on the Promenade, wearing his immaculate suits which, on some days, he changes as many as three times.

From an unsigned article, *Evenings with Leoš Janáček*, which appeared in the magazine, *Dalibor*, Vol. XXVIII (1905—1906, p. 227).

66. FOLK SINGING IN PARTS

I have discovered something entirely new and peculiar in folk music. Perhaps the best name for it would be "Nocturne". They are strange songs for more than one voice to which the people have given unusual harmonies. On my wanderings through the country I heard them in regions so far unexplored. I have no words to describe them.

In the evening, after sunset, the girls gather in the yard. The one with the best voice stands in front of the others and sings. The others then join in, holding hands and standing close together; their song is most strange and seems to spread out over the hill-tops, down into the valley and, in the distance, dissolve into the water flowing through the dark forests.

Leoš Janáček in the above number of the magazine, *Dalibor*.

67. PIANO ACCOMPANIMENTS TO FOLK SONGS

The most enjoyable event was the Moravian folk Nocturnes; a series of folk songs for two women's voices which breathed forth an atmosphere of warm summer nights. Janáček's arrangements which adhere faithfully, both in harmony and in style to the original, are masterly examples of folk song treatment. One is bound to add that the songs gained depth of feeling and were in themselves of so interesting and rare a type that the wish to hear them again was general.

Karel Sázavský

Janáček's *Folk Nocturnes* were performed at a musical evening of the Friends of Art Club on the 5th December, 1907. The critique appeared in *Dalibor*, Vol. XXX, (1907—1908, p. 91). — *Karel Sázavský* (1858—1930), Czech music critic and writer on music.

68. RHAPSODIC FORM IN THE DANCES OF MORAVIAN SLOVAKIA

I am engaged in studying national songs and dances. From these collections we may deduct certain rules which can be made valid for composing, if our music is to remain truly Czech in character. Our national dances could also influence it from the point of view of harmony, use of key and, above all, form. (The use of musical form.) I have been collecting national dances in Moravia for three years. So far, I have become acquainted with that part of Eastern Moravia which comprises Hukvaldy (Čeladná, Kunčice, Tichá, Mniší, Sklenov, Rychaltice, Kozlovice). My ballet *Rákoš Rákoczsy* is one of the results of these studies. During my last journey to Moravian Slovakia I specialized in the dances, mainly the one called *Danaj*, surprising for its rhapsodic form. Naturally the products of Southern Moravia, even the dances, vary considerably from those of the poor Wallachian country. Collecting, or rather, the avoidance of all further delay in collecting national dances in Moravia, should become our sacred duty.

From Janáček's request of the 17th November, 1891 to the Czech Academy of Art and Science in Prague, for financial assistance while studying national dances.

69. HIS FIRST SUCCESS IN PRAGUE

Today's rehearsal of *Rákoš Rákoczy* made a great impression on all those present. The ballet shows promise of being a great success. It is the first experiment in national Slavonic ballet. *Rákoš Rákoczy* is Janáček's magnificent orchestration of Wallachian dances in the beautiful arrangement of Mr. Berger.

The first performance was a great success. The house was sold out, and the applause tremendous. The curtain had to be raised six times.

Reports on the ballet, *Rákoš Rákóczy*, from the magazine, *Moravské listy*, Vol. III, 29th July, 1891. The ballet came into being in the spring of 1891 by combining Wallachian and Hanakian dances for mixed chorus and soloists, to a libretto by Jan Herben. The first performance took place at the Prague National Theatre on the 24th July, 1891. — *August Berger* (1861—1945), choreographer of the Prague National Theatre.

70. HARMONIZATIONS OF FOLK SONGS FROM HIS BIRTH-PLACE

Leoš Janáček, being the director of the Brno school of music, lives in the midst of the Moravian people. As was shown by his music to the ballet, *Rákoš Rákóczy*, he is exploring the unfathomable waters of Moravian folk poetry and music. Now he has published a collection of thirteen Wallachian songs which he himself discovered and for which he has composed piano accompaniments. Here Janáček sets out to make piano arrangements in the original peasant style where the voice is accompanied either by the cymbalom or in combination with other village players. In this he has been remarkably successful even if this cannot be said of the accompaniment from the pianistic point of view. He has even succeeded in suggesting the unusual harmonic combinations, and has reproduced the uneven rhythms which are entirely independent of the metronome and are completely unrestrained. Janáček has given each song its own original aspect, and comes as near as possible to the true spirit of these songs by resisting the temptation to introduce any elements foreign to the style of this particular folk music.

The above critique, which appeared in *Dalibor*, Vol. XXI, 1898—1899, p. 44, is concerned with Janáček's arrangements of thirteen folk songs from his birthplace.

71. PREPARATIONS FOR THE ETHNOGRAPHICAL EXHIBITION IN PRAGUE

Our life here in Moravia will be, until the time of the exhibition, a series of preparatory shows. It is necessary for the players to play together so that they may acquire a more harmonious and pleasant tone. I think it inadvisable, however, to study any kind of fixed programme with them. Even at the exhibition, the songs and dances should be chosen and improvised on the spur of the moment. Yet the performances must be guided by a strong and experienced hand. So far, the results from the preparatory exhibitions of Frenštát, Vsetín, and Hodonín are very promising. The organizers, together with the advisory committee for Moravia, should be able to present a complete, true and pleasing picture of folk music in Moravia.

From Janáček's article on the Ethnographical Exhibition in Prague published in *Lidové Noviny*, 10th June, 1894. — *Frenštát* and *Vsetín*, towns in Moravian Wallachia, and *Hodonín*, a town in Moravian Slovakia, organized local ethnographical exhibitions during 1892—1893.

72. JANÁČEK THE ORGANIZER

It is necessary that not only composers who are living in Moravia, but also Pavel Křížkovský and Förchtgott-Tovačovský should have their works performed. It is, first and foremost, a question for consideration by Moravian singing societies. Away with those dreamers! Let them be ashamed to let such names be neglected. Křížkovský means for Brno what his pupils mean for Western Moravia. Let all these unenterprising societies take the following slogan: encourage and practise choral works, especially those of Křížkovský. In Olomouc and in Eastern Moravia, let them sing Tovačovský. From the works of these two masters and from other composers living in Moravia, it would be possible to compile three interesting programmes which could be used with excellent results at the exhibition in Prague. These matters will be the special responsibility of Mr. Nešvera and Mr. Sázavský, both of whom are members of the advisory council for Moravia. In the same way, the group sponsored by the magazine, *Cyril*, will find many opportunities of singing religious folk songs successfully. I should like to draw attention to the sixteenth-century composer Jacob Handl who was choir-master at Olomouc. This side of the work will be organized by Dr Kolísek. I dare not do more than whisper my hope that the National Theatre in Brno may even perform operas by Moravian composers dealing with subjects from Moravian history. If all these points were attended to, Moravia could be excellently represented at the exhibition in eight or ten unusually interesting programmes which would be devoted entirely to music.

From Janáček's article on the Ethnographical Exhibition in Prague which appeared in *Lidové Noviny*, 14th June, 1894. — *Arnošt Förchtgott-Tovačovský* (1825—1874), Czech composer from the Hanakian town of Tovačov. He became a fervent patriot in Vienna. — *Josef Nešvera* (1842—1914) Czech composer who grew up among Moravian folk music and, in 1884, became choir-master at the main church of Olomouc. — *Karel Sázavský*, see note on page 75 — *Jacob Handl* (1550—1591), Slovenian composer who was from 1580 to 1585 choir-master to the Bishop of Olomouc. — *Dr František Kolísek* was in charge of the Moravian section of the Ethnographical Exhibiton in Prague.

73. FROM FOLK SONG TO COMPOSING

The fact that there are over 3000 folk songs in general use in Moravia, all of them purely national in character and interesting in type, fills me with joy. I am not concerned so much with their value as collection pieces. They are mainly a means of understanding life as long as they remain an aesthetic criterion. They are the unity of song with the hardships of life.

A song cut off from the life of the people is a puzzle. Only from living song can music of the same style develop. I therefore believe that by encouraging scientific research, the knowledge of folk song forms will penetrate into our composers' work, especially as the continuity of such development has never been interrupted. We link up with the playing and composing of the village players Kotka, Manka, Peterka, Klepáč, Lhoťan, Trn and Uhelný.

From Janáček's article, *Thoughts While Travelling*, published in *Dalibor*, No. 29, 1906–1907, pp. 189 ff.

74. FEELINGS FOR RUSSIA

Janáček's whole personality was in sympathy with Slavonic and Russian tendencies. His birthplace, East Lachia, was a kind of bridge between Western Czechoslovakia and the neighbouring Poland and Russia. In Russia, he saw a protector for the smaller Slavonic nations. His family connections played an important part in his leanings towards Russia. Two of his brothers, František and Josef, lived there for many years. Josef's children settled there for good. Janáček's nephew, Vladimír, lived in Volynia. A second nephew, Leo, lived in the Ukraine near Kharkov and his niece Olga lived in Moscow.

In 1878 Janáček had wanted to study at the Petersburg conservatoire, in order to attend Anton Rubinstein's master-class. Janáček heard Rubinstein in Prague and in Leipzig, where he became his ardent disciple and made him his idol until the year 1880. During that year, he began intensive studies of Tchaikovký's music, which he conducted in Brno. He wrote about it in the magazine, "Hudební Listy", which he had founded, and also in the paper, "Moravské Listy". For Janáček, Tchaikovsky was a composer of extensive ideas, an excellent writer of counterpoint of the Berlioz school, with a great knowledge of many musical forms. At that time Janáček also did much to spread Russian literature, especially after the year 1900, when he had already travelled there consider-

9. A scene from the Jubilee performance of *Jenufa* at the Janáček Opera House in Brno (1954, 50 years after its first performance). In the centre: Kostelnička, (Marie Steinerová) and Jenufa (Libuše Domaninská).

10. The Beseda House, to-day the Army House, with the memorial of the worker, František Pavlík, killed during a demonstration. His death inspired Janáček to write his cycle of piano compositions, *The Street Scene*.

ably. (1896 and 1902.) Janáček followed the example of his artistic adviser and friend, Dvořák, in his interest in Slavonic matters. He refreshed his strength and gained new artistic inspiration from his knowledge of the Russian people and their literature. At the height of his creative activities immediately after World War I, he alternated Russian and Czech themes as inspiration for his works.

From my article entitled *Janáček and Tchaikovsky* (*Almanac for Students of Philosophy at the Masaryk University, Brno* 1953).

75. HIS ESTIMATION OF SLAVONIC FOLK SONGS

Janáček's opinions of Slavonic music are surprising. He states them in his magazine, "Hudební Listy", published in the year 1887, while under the influence of Ludvík Kuba's magnificent collection of Slavonic folk songs which appeared under the title, "The Slavs Seen Through Their Songs".

Janáček wrote: To compile a book of folk songs of all the Slavonic nations, is a gigantic task if we are to do it truly and honourably, and deserves great merit. When comparing the songs of the various Slavonic nations we begin to realise, for the first time, the full meaning of Slavonic folk music. I am convinced that in time, a classical Slavonic music will arise, which will know no divisions into Czech, Russian and so on. And again he wrote: Just as the Roman chant has had, for so many centuries, such a strong influence on the development of Western European music, I am convinced that the Slavonic folk song will have the same strong influence on musical composition of the future.

In this, we cannot entirely agree with Janáček. It is impossible to create classical Slavonic music, just as it is impossible to create a combined classical Slavonic language. The creation of so-called Slavonic music, for example, by comparing the musical form of the folk songs, would be artificial and strained. Janáček showed, in his own music, that his art was firmly rooted in his homeland Bohemia and Moravia, and grew out of its folk songs and dances.

From my essay on the problems of Slavonic music in Czechoslovakia (*Slavism in Czech National Life*, Brno, 1947). — *Ludvík Kuba* (1863—) one of the foremost Czech painters, a concientious collector and editor of folk songs, and a composer.

76. CRITICISM OF THE OPERA *EUGEN ONEGIN*

Beautiful and refined music. Everyone, whether layman or artist, would certainly have expressed themselves in this way after hearing the opera *Eugen Onegin*, by Tchaikovsky. The music in the second scene is of special interest to us, because of its aptness of character. That spiritual excitement which at one moment engulfs us and the next moment carries us on its passion to giddy heights and an athmosphere of elation, is achieved in the music with great mastery. In Gremin's aria on love a normal ternary form is used. The long, deep notes above which the orchestra flows on, is a masterly stroke. The rhythm of the melody strongly resembles the rhythm of the spoken word. The rhythmical style makes no allowance for independent melodic subjects and countersubjects. All the characters, Onegin, Tatiana, Olga and Lenski, sing in the same style. If we interchanged their parts, the difference would scarcely be observed. They all sing in the same way, beautifully, but nothing more. This is the main fault of Tchaikovsky's lyrical scenes. The melodies have no rhythmical differentiation.

From Janáček's critique of the performance of *Eugen Onegin* in Brno (*Moravské listy*, 28th February 1891).

77. HIS ADMIRATION FOR THE OPERA
THE QUEEN OF SPADES

The music of Tschaikovsky's opera in three acts and seven scenes, the Q u e e n   o f   S p a d e s, is music of horror! Agitated, fragmentary, without being bound in any way by broad melodies. The orchestra seems to beat up a succession of uncertain pricking sounds. And yet, after all, it joins maturely the highest thoughts of the composer—all these small pieces into a magnificient whole, with such surprising results as few world—famous works have so far achieved. W e l l d e v i s e d themes and u n p r e m e d i t a t e d themes... both are deeply felt; a second truth is born without the theoretical meaning being immediately clear to the composer. Strange forces control the whole spirit and make us blush. Waves of melody, of varying dimensions, either contract or expand according to the situation. The harmonic background, however, never loses its main character. This method of composing is peculiar to Mr. Tchaikovsky, and protects him, even when writing works which have no connection with words: symphonies and overtures.

How the spirit of Russian folk music brightens up the other-wise gloomy atmosphere! We hear the chorus of village maidens: "Oh my dearest Mashenka..." or the chorus: "Her Ladyship tired herself at the ball..." or the chorus in the gambling den: "In wind and rain we gamble..." The first, brimming over with devilry, the second, with heart-felt melody, and the third, with an uneven rhythm such as is found in Moravian dances; three bars of $\frac{2}{4}$ followed by two bars of $\frac{3}{4}$. The composer, who was able to write the ball scene (Act 2, Scene 3) in 18th century style, must surely have roots deep in the folk music of his country, enabling him to write these three pearls of absolute music.

It is high time for the air to be cleared in musical Brno. We have had too long a spell of almost complete suffocation. Once more a truly artistic work enlightened the scene. The genius of originality, sincerity of style and musical truth was once more before us. To this we should cling, and to it lead our art. For these reasons, the first performance of the *Queen of Spades* in the Czech Theatre in Brno, on the 16th January, 1896, must be regarded as a day of the utmost importance.

Article in *Lidové Noviny*, 21st January, 1896, which Janáček wrote before setting out on his jurney to Russia to visit the All Russia Exhibition of Industry and Art in Nizhny Novgorod. This was also the criticism of the first performance of the *Queen of Spades* in the Czech National Theatre in Brno on June 16th, 1896.

78. IMPRESSIONS FROM RUSSIA

Nature has allotted us this place
for carving out a window into Europe...
says Peter the Great in Pushkin's poem *(Petersburg)*. Through this window, so many foreign elements were brought to Russia, that finally even we Czechs begin to use it in the normal historical way. This year, with the closing of the German theatre, excellent concerts are being organized in the Pavlovsk railway station by Mr. Galkin, a professor of the Petersburg Conservatoire. The railway tickets also permit one to hear the concerts, which vary in type from day to day. One day in each week is devoted to Russian composers. Every Friday is a full–scale symphony concert. On the 12th of "Yulja" according to the old Russian calendar, the eighth symphony concert was dedicated to the memory of Anton Rubinstein. The following of his works were performed: 1. *Ivan the Terrible*, symphonic poem. 2. Second Cello Concerto. 3. Songs. 4. Fourth Piano Concerto. 5. Fourth Symphony.

The symphonic poem *Ivan the Terrible* is loquacious; luckily, it was well played. The third movement of the Cello Concerto appeals to me on account of its folk song character. The same may be said for the Piano Concerto, at the end of which Rubinstein breaks out in a truly "voice of the people" style which remains as the "music of God". The 'cellist, Mr. Edvard Jakobs, played cleanly and steadily. But who cares for icy beauty! I want to hear in each note that it has done more than merely pass through the player's fingers, that it comes from the heart. The pianist, Mr. Gollidej, and the conductor, Mr. Galkin, fell out with each other over the last movement of the piano concerto. I realize that my advice comes too late, but the conductor should have conducted the $\frac{2}{4}$ bar in one and Mr. Gollidej should know that even in strict time, we play to the end...

Leoš Janáček: Some Remarks from Holiday Travels III. Janáček wrote about his first journey to Russia (18th July to 2nd August, 1896) in three articles which appeared in *Lidové Noviny* on the 2nd and 15th August and on the 8th September, 1896. — *Nicholai Vladimirovich Galkin* (1850—1906), Russian conductor and violinist.

79. RUSSIAN CHURCH CHOIRS

It is generally known that Russian church choirs are magnificent. And truly it is bliss for a musician to listen to them. The ceremony, from the musical point of view, is a perfect whole. The choir sings the responses with unusual lightness, in long pianissimos which they hold over while the priest, exactly in tune, continues with the prayer. No interruptions, no pauses; no startling modulations. The clear spirit of the music is never allowed to attract unnecessary attention to itself, nor distract one's thoughts from the ceremony. The peaceful, almost inaudible notes of the choir, make a striking contrast to the full—voiced tone of the priest. I am now convinced that the ungainly German stops in our organs are a godless roar.

Petersburg, 30th July, 1896.

Leoš Janáček: Some Remarks from Holiday Travels II. From Janáček's article which appeared in *Lidové Noviny*, 15th August, 1896.

80. IMPRESSIONS FROM PETERSBURG

If you want a picture of Petersburg, you must see Prague in your mind's eye. Příkopy and Ferdinand Street are not unlike the Nevsky Prospect, where streams of people, from all walks of life, throng the street from early morning till late at night. From left and right they pour into the main street from the adjoining Ligovska Street which cuts across the beginning of the Nevsky Prospect from the East side and which resembles our Dělnická Street. Here are many factories and large work-shops of the most varied kinds. Along the middle of the street, the former Ligovsky Canal is now a shady row of trees which in three places broadens out into "Children's Plantations." What a crowd of youngsters play here in the sand! Here they are certainly safe, for the play-grounds are surrounded by high iron railings. Not even a dog can get through to worry them. On each side of the trees, is the noisy thorough-fare with its stone surface. The pavements in front of the houses are also paved with broad slabs of stone. There is cleanliness along the whole length of the street, as it is the duty of every janitor to sweep and water the road in front of his house. A hydrant rises out of the pavement in front of every building. The street is swept and watered very often. Another health measure which appealed to me very much are the tubs filled with boiled, cooled water which stand in front of every inn. There is no other drinking water. It is the duty of the inn-keeper to provide fresh, cooled water, and the duty of the "Gradavoi" (town policeman) to see that the water is really fresh.

Petersburg "looks into Europe" from the five branches of the river Neva; from the North they are as follows, Neva, Malaya Neva, Malaya, Srednaya and Bolshaya Nevska. Close to the Admiralty is the landing stage, or pier, for steamers sailing in the direction of Kronstadt and Peterhof, the summer palace of the Czar. We go on board the steamer which will sail in a few minutes for Peterhof. We sail into the gulf. Petersburg sinks down behind us into the ripples of the sea, leaden in colour. We are in the gulf of Finland.

I am the second person to bring back water from the Baltic sea to my native village. The first was Jan Čapek of Sány and Hukvaldy, a Hussite captain.

Petersburg, 26th July, 1896.

Leoš Janáček: Remarks from Holiday Travels I. From Janáček's article which appeared in Lidové Noviny, 2nd August, 1896. — Jan Čapek of Sány and Hukvaldy, a Hussite captain of the first half of the 15th century, reached Danzig during his roamings as a warrior.

81. ADMIRATION FOR MOSCOW

The Kremlin — great God! What a fairy-tale. So intimate and endearing with its many blue, green and other coloured towers. Inside — and round about, a beautiful view. Moscow seen from here is a sea of towers — there are sixteen hundred of them.

I am so glad that I stayed here longer. Otherwise I would have missed the nicest part of my travels. But now I must take leave of beloved Russia. How it grieves me. It is so nice here.

From the essay The Spiritual Workshop of Leoš Janáček. (Brno, 1936) by Jan Racek (born 1905), Professor of Musicology at the Masaryk University in Brno, and editor of Janáček's correspondence and literary work.

82. SOCIAL CONCEPTION OF THE CANTATA OUR FATHER

On his journeys to Russia, Janáček visited Poland, which was then incorporated in the Czarist Empire. Janáček made a point of visiting Warsaw. Here he felt as though he were in Moravia and was particularly attracted by the folk music. He wrote about Polish music in the Brno paper, "Lidové Noviny", carried on correspondence with Polish authors, knew and studied continually the works of the greatest Polish composer, Chopin. Janáček keenly studied

Chopin's harmony and melody, and expressed his admiration for Chopin's masterliness. Often he went out of his way to remark on Chopin's refined sense of form which was so admirably suited to the piano. He considered his harmonic sense to be of very high potentiality and fully realised the energetic and even heroic content of some of Chopin's compositions. Janáček was probably the only musician in Brno at the end of the 19th Century who was thoroughly familar with Polish culture. This is very evident in his musical illustrations to the cycle of paintings, "O u r F a t h e r", by the Polish painter, Josef Krzesz-Mecina. Janáček was captivated by the rich colours of the cycle; nevertheless, he protested in his music against the idealised conception of *Our Father*, by shifting the musical centre of interest towards mankind. Here, once more, we have proof of his realistic understanding of life. Christianity was for him an offensive in the fight for existence. So much so, that one might almost call it socialism. Man has the right to exist and Janáček demandéd that this right be respected.

From my essay entitled *Janáček and Poland*, (*Collected Essays in Philosophy of the Masaryk University, Brno* 1954). — *Josef Krzesz-Męcina* (1860—1934), pupil of Jan Matějka, devoted himself to painting religious subjects. His cycle *Our Father* was printed in the Polish paper *Tygodnik Illustrovany* in 1899. *Our Father* is written for mixed choir, tenor, organ and harp, and originated in 1901.

83. AGAINST FALSE CRITICISM

Dear Sir,

I have often said, and it is also generally known, that my *Our Father* is not intended to do more than represent what is in Krzesz's pictures. Why was this not taken into account? On the concert platform, this was lost to the audience. Perhaps the pictures should have been printed in the programme. I was not consulted. But why do you and Mr. Zázvorka wrong me so? In Brno the work was sung to tableaux-vivant — still remembered as an unforgettable performance. Forgive me for complaining, but I feel sure that you will agree that every work must be performed as the composer intended, and that it should be judged also from that point of view.

I remain yours very respectfully,

Leoš Janáček.

18th November, 1906.

A letter to *Dr Jan Branberger* (1877—1952), editor of the magazine *Smetana*, where the critic Dr B. Zázvorka published an unfavorable review of *Our Father* and its performance in Prague in 1906. This work was originally written as incidental music to tableaux-vivant.

84. DIRECTOR OF THE WARSAW CONSERVATOIRE?

Janáček's sympathetic understanding of Polish culture, his pioneer activities at the Organ School, his theoretical work, his interesting activity in collecting and studying folk songs and dances, and his conducting and composing and organizing ability, made itself known abroad, especially in Russia and in Poland, where Janáček had travelled. It is possible that his cantata *Our Father* inspired by Krzesz's cycle of pictures, was responsible for awakening interest in him in Poland. This all added to Janáček's great importance, especially when, in the year 1904, he was offered the post of Director of the Warsaw Conservatoire, where Chopin had received his training. At that time, Janáček was busily employed in the preparations for the performance of his opera, *Jenufa*, in Brno, and was obliged to postpone any decision. However, in May of that year, he travelled to Warsaw to discuss the terms in person. He did not become director of the Warsaw Conservatoire, mainly on account of the political situation at the time of the Russo-Japanese war. He preferred to work at home in Brno for the furtherance of Czech national culture, as director of the Organ School. He remained faithful to himself.

From my essay, *Janáček and Poland*, (Collected Essays in Philosophy of the Masaryk University, Brno 1954).

85. STUDYING THE MELODIC AND DRAMATIC ACCENTS OF FOLK SPEECH

Melodic curves of speech? For me, music emanating from instruments, whether in the works of Beethoven or of any other composer, contains little real truth. You see, with me it was always odd. When anyone speaks to me, I listen more to the tonal modulations in his voice than to what he is actually saying. From this, I know at once what he is like, what he feels, whether he is lying, whether he is agitated or whether he is merely making conventional conversation. I can even feel, or rather hear, any hidden sorrow. Life is sound, the tonal modulations of the human speech. Every living creation is filled with the deepest truth. That, you see, has been one of the main needs of my life. I have been taking down speech melodies since the year '97. I have a vast collection of notebooks filled with them—you see, they are my window through which I look into the soul—but this is what I should like to emphasize: they are of the utmost importance to dramatic music.

From an interview with Janáček which appeared in the magazine, *Literární svět*, Vol. I, 1928. (Prague, the 8th March.)

86. THE MELODIC CURVES OF SPEECH UNVEILING THE SPIRIT

The melodic curves of speech are an expression of the complete organism and of all phases of its spiritual activities. They demonstrate whether a man is stupid or intelligent, sleepy or awake, tired or alert. They tell us whether he is a child or an old man, whether it is morning or evening, light or darkness, heat or frost, and disclose whether a person is alone or in company. The art of dramatic writing is to compose a melodic curve which will, as if by magic, reveal immediately a human being in one definite phase of his existence.

From Janáček's article, *Last Year, This Year*, which appeared in the magazine, *Hlídka*, No. XXII, 1905, p. 206.

87. MELODIC CURVES OF THE CHILD'S SPEECH

How I love the children who are playing about me at this moment! Their laughter and innocent games, their roguery which always ends in tears. The life here in the meadow is for them a paradise. The morning sun, scented with ripening fruit, kisses them. The lime-trees cast a shimmering afternoon shade for them. At midday, the inquisitive sun seeks them out. I want to preserve a picture of a single afternoon with something more faithful than mere words: with notes. How unusual; I beg you, do not sing the phrases I have taken down in notes; enunciate them in such a way that the notes may indicate the modulations of speech. They will take on a beautiful serenity. You would recognize the children on meeting them and fall in love with them.

From Janáček's article *Elisabeth* which appeared in the *Moravian National Reader* edited by František Bílý and published by the Moravo-Silesian Society in Prague, 1910, pp. 341—347.

88. A PLAN FOR A MUSICAL DICTIONARY OF THE CZECH LANGUAGE

We need a book on the ordinary melodic curves of speech in order to preserve the sound of the Czech language for future generations. It would be a dictionary in notes of the living Czech language, which would contain melodic phrases for everything

which the Czech language is able to express. Let me give an example:
When Mrs. Uprka painted my wooden chest, she discussed the
colours:

She painted:

Mí - ša - né   ty   bar - vy
[Those mixed colours]

Her conversation was quiet and peaceful; I did not want to
disturb her in her work. These are what I would call normal melodic
curves of speech. Here there is no annoyance, no bitterness, no
anger, no gaiety, no sadness. They are pronounced almost without
any alternations and accents, whether used in the morning or
before going to bed. Whoever you may meet, will tell you the
name of the parish in the same way. Which shows how the melodic
curves of speech are general.

The ordinary melodic curve of a name does not beg nor com-
mand nor flatter. It is an echo of the name of every object which
has been passed on over the centuries. Its correct pronunciation
pleases the ear, while its deformation through the mouth of
a foreigner offends us. It is the treasure of the language—an unnoticed treasure. There is an elementary proportion in the length
of individual sounds which agrees with the natural length of the
vowels and consonants. Every idiom arranges itself in its own way
and yet it is understandable to the whole nation. Everyone makes
his contribution. This specific intonation is typical for each age,
each generation—each group of persons.

Such melodic curves of speech are expressed in certain octaves
and in definite intervals. They are an inherent quality of man;
his normal speech. One can neither hide them
nor conceal them,—to disown them would
mean to change the colour and texture of
the voice—of the melodic curves of speech.

The i n d i v i d u a l quality of the normal melodic curves of speech is as much typical for them as their natural production.

They fall into the nearest surroundings for which they are destined. They shun the crowd; the noise and bustle of cities. They are of a nonchalant, rather than of a self-conscious character. They were created in a spirit of healthy life which they will never forsake.

From Leoš Janáček's article *The Border-Line of Speech and Song*, published in the magazine *Hlídka*, Vol. XXIII, Brno, 1906, No. 4. — *Anežka Úprka*, wife of the Czech painter, Joža Úprka (1861—1940), a friend of Janáček.

89. MELODIC CURVES OF SPEECH FROM THE BRNO STREETS

The best way of becoming a good opera composer is to study analytically the melodic curves and contours of human speech. Only in this way can one get to know the inexhaustible fund of true patterns for dramatic, melodic curves of speech in the Czech language. These phrases, if observed only when set in songs, are not so alive and pregnant with meaning. That is to say, they contain less freedom of modulation in the voice than is necessary for dramatic music. The melodic curves of speech, as used in song, give only a reflection of the spirit weakened by the heat of the music. But the melodic curves of speech as used in the spoken word, are a direct reflex of life. If, however, they have an insufficiently dramatic elasticity when in song, there will certainly be none in the harshly hewn prose of the literary language. Let us observe some examples of the melodic curves of speech from the streets of Brno.

A mischievous factory girl calls across the street to some other factory girls:

[Whom are you waiting for?]

An old public servant complains in a hoarse, drunken voice:

My ne - má - me   co   dě - lat
[We have nothing to do.]

From desperation he even breaks into song.

A worse picture of poverty is a deserted beggar, who goes into the Beseda house carrying a pot of kitchen waste. In a harsh, angry voice he complains to a woman even worse-looking than himself:

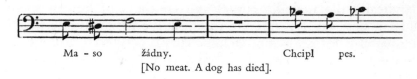

Ma - so   žádny.   Chcipl   pes.
[No meat. A dog has died].

A little boy of about four years old wants to attract the attention of another small boy and calls out:

Poď sém,   poď sém!   Já ti   ně - co   po - vím
[Come here, come here! I will tell you something]

A former student greets his professor in a breezy, friendly way:

Dobrý   ve - čer!
[Good evening!]

94

And once more:

Do - brý   ve - čer!

[Good evening!]

He passes a girl carrying a pail of water and, looking into her eyes, greets her familiarly:

Dó - bry   ve - čer!

[Good evening!]

A factory-hand and a factory girl part unwillingly. After a few steps, they turn round and the girl, encouraged by the way he looks at her, calls back, softly:

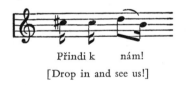

Přindi k   nám!

[Drop in and see us!]

The girl, with movements like a young gazelle, hurries away from her companions:

Já   mu - sím   it   dom,   já   mám   hlad!

[I must go home, I'm hungry!]

The word, "home" sounds like a bell which probably reminds her of happy reunions. The other girls eye her with distrust.

An old woman calls out to a hawker:

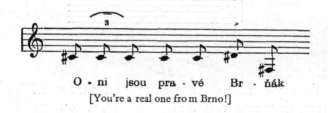

Mes - li - te, že zme jak Br - ňá - ci?
[Do you think we are like these Brno people?]

Brno probably has a bad reputation among the people; a worker calls out:

O - ni jsou pra - vé Br - ňák
[You're a real one from Brno!]

90. ROSA NEWMARCH ON JANÁČEK

Janáček believes that folk songs were often the joint product of a group of exceptionally talented people and proceeded from their receptivity and power of imitation. For him, "the folk song is a living cell, and even its fragments are endowed with vitality and mobility: it has been, and can continue to be, modified; it has decayed—and still decays—on the lips of unintelligent and irreverent singers. ... Song lives by, and in, speech; the whole spirit of the Czech people is manifested in their speech; to every word

11. Karel Kovařovic, who conducted the first performance of *Jenufa* at the National Theatre in Prague.

12. Dr. Max Brod, a well known propagator of Janáček's work.

they utter is attached a fragment of the national life... Therefore the melody of the people's speech should be studied in every detail.".... "It seems," he says, "that for individual musical characterization—especially opera—these melodic fragments from daily life are of the greatest significance. By them we shall hit on the truth; we shall grasp how the human individual utters words of love; with what intensity he expresses his hate; we shall discover the melodic curve of energy; we shall hear how tenderly is rounded off the phrase which comes from the goodness of a woman's heart." And elsewhere he says: "On the stage, it is not always the best word for vocalising that we require; we need the every-day word, its melodic turn, torn from life, misery congealed, despair in sharp relief. Real life is needed in opera."

From *Rosa Newmarch's* essay entitled *Leoš Janáček and Moravian Music-Drama. The Slavonic Review* 1922—1923. *Rosa Newmarch* (1857—1940), British writer on music and a great propagator of Czech music.

91. OBJECTIONS TO ARIAS AND LEITMOTIVE

Opera is the combination of several arts. The opera composer must concentrate on many things and for this reason opera has always been regarded as the peak of creative art. The history of opera is the mother of wisdom. Gluck, Mozart, Wagner and the modern composers have always tried to present the truth on the stage. That is to say, real people and not caricatures, in fact real life and not a caricature of life. In Smetana, there is more variety than in Wagner. The fact that people do not think but speak in real life makes it necessary to avoid placing arias and songs in opera where they would not occur in real life. Here we come to the importance of the melodic curves of speech.

Leoš Janáček as quoted by *Václav Kaprál* in an article on Janáček's relationship to opera, which appeared in the magazine, *Hudební rozhledy*, Vol. I, 1924—1925, pp. 63 ff. *Václav Kaprál* (1889—1947), professor at the Brno Conservatoire, studied under Janáček at the Organ School in the year 1909.

92. *JENUFA* AND THE MELODIC CURVES OF SPEECH

At the time when I was writing *Jenufa* I became absorbed in the question of the melodic curves and contours of speech. Not according to the example of my famous forerunners, but by listening to the speech of passers-by. I read the expressions in their faces and in their eyes. I roamed through the back streets and observed the surroundings of the speakers; their type of society, time, light, dusk, cold and warmth. I felt all the indications which the melodic curves of their speech threw into sharp relief. The variety of this word-music is boundless. Here, shining forth and dissolving; there, hardening and piercing. But I was also able to feel something far deeper than the mere melody of the speech, something which had remained hidden. I felt that the word-melodies were traces of hidden currents within the self. From them I could catch sadness, snatches of gaiety, determination, indecision, etc. In short, I felt, in the melodic curves of speech "spiritual problems". I was afforded great pleasure by the beauty of the phrases, by the comprehensiveness and sufficiency of their expression. I could see further into the depths of the soul of a person if I listened to the melodic curves and contours of his speech.

From Janáček's article on *Jenufa*, which appeared in the magazine, *Hudební Revue*, Vol. IX, 1915—1916, pp. 245—249.

93. Mrs. JANÁČEK ON *JENUFA*

The central point of Janáček's creative work is his opera, *Jenufa*, with libretto by Gabriela Preiss, a work into which he poured all his pain and love. His remark about it is well known: "*Jenufa* is tied up with the black ribbon of the long illness, pains and cries of my daughter Olga, and my little boy Vladimír." Janáček wrote on the title page of *Jenufa*: "*In memory of my daughter Olga.*"

After the completion of *Jenufa* Janáček sent the opera to the National Theatre in Prague. The director of the opera, Karel Kova-řovic, refused it and gave as his reason that there were technical faults in the score. Janáček's faith in himself as an artist was deeply shaken, but he held his own. Mrs. Janáček remembers the scene: "We were in the room where Olga was dying. My husband sat at his desk and suddenly clutched his head in his hands and tears started streaming down his face. In this sharp fit of depression, he began to blame himself for knowing nothing. This was more than I could stand. I had always believed in him as an artist, and I believed especially in the beauty and greatness of *Jenufa*. I took his head in my arms and, crying myself, tried to comfort him. My great faith in his work enabled me to find the right words of comfort. They must have been convincing because he gradually calmed himself. After that, I kept watch over him so as to avoid the recurrence of such a shock."

From *Helfert's* article entitled, *Mrs. Zdeňka Janáček* (*Tempo* No. XVII, 1937—1938, p. 15). Janáček completed his opera, *Jenufa*, on the 18th March, 1903. He worked on it from 1894, but most intensively in the years 1902—1903 during the time of his daughter's serious illness which resulted in her death.

94. ILLNESS OF HIS DAUGHTER OLGA

I now see clearly before me the whole of your sad case. Do not worry yourself by contemplating your misfortune and do not lose faith in yourself. This does not mean that you are unfortunate. On the contrary: the small, weak beetle climbs up to the top of a tall tree and gratifies his spirit with a view of the world. Take him for your example. I fear, dearest one, that you are again very ill. Do not lose faith in yourself. With what torment I await news of you. It is much harder than you think for me to bear the misery of your life. Send me your greetings, my little girl. I am with you in my thoughts. Once more I am condemned to bear such a tragic fate, but I will banish it a hundred times over. Today's postcard weighs on me like a disaster. And you, my poor one, what you must go through. I am unable to think. I am prepared to take my holiday and come to meet you. To be here or with you—in this awful state of distraction—nothing matters any more.

Extract from Janáček's letters written between the end of May and July 1902 to his daughter Olga who had been staying, since March of that year, in Petersburg. Janáček's brother, František, lived there permanently which accounted for Olga's feeling so at home there. She was suddenly smitten with a serious illness and had to be taken to the Petersburg hospital. In June 1902, Mrs. Janáček travelled out to nurse her daughter and, half way through July, was able to bring her back to Brno. The desperate Janáček, who guessed that his daughter's illness would prove fatal, travelled to Warsaw to meet them on their way.

95. OLGA—THE FIRST TO HEAR *JENUFA*

On Sunday 22nd February, 1903, Miss Olga received extreme unction. She knew that she had little time to live and said, "Daddy, play me your opera, I shan't live to hear it." The master played her the whole opera; and Miss Olga enjoyed listening to it very much. Five days later, 26th February, 1903, she died.

The above are the words of *Marie Stejskal*, faithful servant in the Janáček household.

96. WITHOUT A TITLE

Our Olga is dying and sends her greetings to you for the last time.

Janáček's postcard to *Vincenc Sládek*, forester of Hukvaldy. Without introduction, unsigned, undated. (Post office stamp: Brno, 24th February, 1903.)

97. DEATH OF HIS DAUGHTER

Dear Sládeček and Mrs. Sládeček,

We no longer have her, our dear little heart. What bitter tears she wept when on her death bed she remembered you and your children. My heart wept for her that she should have been condemned to part from us while still in the full bloom of youth and beauty and angelic goodness. How fearfully she suffered! It is impossible to describe. Once again, be so kind as to prepare your room for us, it will be our place of mourning. The Sunday before last, she showed signs of a slight improvement, and, at once, remembered Hukvaldy and the holidays, but on Tuesday she began her death throes. She was so loath to die and we were so loath to lose her. It was as though someone was tearing my heart out, and that is how I continue to feel...

Brno, 7th March, 1903.

From a letter which Janáček wrote to *Vincenc Sládek* and his family. — Seldom was such loneliness and heart-breaking sorrow so strongly expressed as in this letter. With Olga and Janáček's two-year-old son, Vladimír (died 1890), died also his last hope, his last child.

98. NEW HOPES FOR *JENUFA*

Dear Madam,

Yesterday was one of my rare happy days. Perhaps the Almighty has at last decided to turn a smiling face upon me. The management of the National Theatre in Brno sent for the score of my opera, *Jenufa*. When he took it, the clerk certainly carried a great weight on his shoulders; it seemed to me as though he carried many sad years of my life... I will now ask to be pensioned off and so be relieved of my work as Royal Imperial Music Teacher, and be able to devote my entire time to composing and writing. At last I can see times on the horizon for which I have waited my whole life. Shall I live to enjoy them? Will my spirit be able to bear me up in order to do better work? I think so... Although, who can tell what goes on in his own brain? My brain makes my whole body work so wildly; it can be explained only by guessing and astonishment. It is the will of God and fate. We make our own fate ... Here in Brno, I am a poor man—as though in a desert—where there is no proper music to be heard.

From Janáček's letter 9th October, 1903, to Mrs. Kamila Urválek, wife of the forester of Zaháje near Dolní Královice in Bohemia, whom he met at Luhačovice some time during 1903. This excerpt from the letter is here published for the first time.

99. FIRST REHEARSALS OF *JENUFA*

Dear Madam,

I have just returned, completely worn out, from the first full rehearsal of the first act. Such a quarrel broke out between the director and the conductor, that it almost made me afraid. The "trumpeter" was so severely told off during the rehearsal, and took it so much to heart, that he went and got himself into a critical state of drunkenness. He recognized no "authority". Cursed at everyone as though they had been dogs. It was a pebble which brought down an avalanche in its wake—and almost ruined my premiére. With great difficulty, some sort of order was restored so that the rehearsal could be brought to a close. You poor creature, who longed for the life of the theatre, should be only too glad that you are in your present situation.

I am deathly tired. Thin, yellow as a Good Friday candle. My eyes refuse to keep open – but, after all, I seem to be happier. Enclosed you will find something printed which invites you to my celebration. So much has happened to me lately that I am unable to think at all. I was offered the post of Director of the Warsaw Conservatoire. I requested them to postpone their decision, as I am at present unable to deliberate the matter. I spent a day in Prague, as you know from my postcard. God grant that everything will go well on Thursday. I hope you are keeping well, and that your husband will be able to find the time to come here with you.

I am, with deepest respect,

Yours sincerely,

This hitherto unpublished letter to Kamila Urválek was preserved without its envelope and without a date. It can be placed with certainty before the first performance of *Jenufa* in Brno (Thursday, 21st January, 1904) to which performance Janáček invited the Urváleks. He did not discuss the matter of the directorship of the Warsaw Conservatoire until May 1904, when he failed to reach any decision.

100. FIRST PERFORMANCE OF *JENUFA* IN BRNO

The first performance of Jenufa (21st January 1904) was a great success for Janáček and meant the victory of this work. The theatre was packed out. The conductor, Hrazdira, raised his hands and almost immediately, we heard the unusual tones of the xylophone and strings. Soon the curtain went up and on the stage sits Jenufa (Miss Marie Kabeláč) singing of her sorrow: "Evening approaches and Števa does not return..." It was all so new and unlike other operas. No steady flow of symphonic music in the orchestra, only colour effects and above it, on the stage, beautiful and heartfelt song, very true to life in character. Then the Grand-mother appears (Mrs. Věra Pivoňka) then Laca (Staněk Doubravský) with his poisonous accusations. Jano (Miss Kříž) gaily announcing: "Now I know how to read!" The Elder (Karel Beníško) praising Jenufa's beauty: "She carries herself like a sack of poppyseed" and finally announcing that Števa has not been enlisted. The alarm on the stage sends shivers down the audience's spine. Jenufa's happiness clashes with Laca's anger when he hears that Števa was not enlisted.

Now comes the "Kostelnička" (Mrs. Hanus-Svoboda) and to her are added the voices of the recruits in the distance: "All get married..."

They finally burst on to the stage in the full beauty of Moravian peasant costume; singing and playing fiddles; the young men, dancing; among them, a whole head taller than the rest, Števa (Bohdan Procházka, later Theodor Schütz of the National Theatre in Prague). The lively fun soon convinced us all that a slice of real life of the Moravian people had been put on the stage, complete with its naturalness and truth. Already, after the first act, the applause was very great and Janáček, who was standing in the wings, had to take a call. He was pale and nervous. The deeply-felt music of the second act with its lyrical mood, made the same deep impression on the audience. The "Kostelnička" of Mrs. Hanus-Svoboda was excellent, and the success of this act even greater than that of the first. Janáček was again called but this time looked happier; he smiled, a proof that he was aware of his success. The dramatic climax in the third act containing the wedding scene which ends in the discovery of the murder of the child (The Village Elder sung by Alois Pivoňka, his wife, Emma Kučera, his daughter Karolka, Růžena Kasper), and finally Laca confessing his love for Jenufa, was a sensational success. There was no end to the clapping. Janáček was called again and again on to the stage; as was also the librettist, Mrs. Preiss, from her box. The students were wildly enthusiastic and accompanied Janáček as far as the Beseda house where a friendly reception was held.

From *Jan Kunc's* article: *Memories of the First Night of Jenufa*, which appeared in the County Theatre Magazine, (*Divadelní List Zemského divadla v Brně*, No. IX, 1933—1934, pp. 78—80). — *Cyril Metoděj Hrazdira* (1868—1926), Janáček's pupil, conductor and composer. The first to conduct *Jenufa*. — *Gabriela Preiss* (1862—1946), Czech writer. She wrote the libretto for Foerster's opera *Eva* as well as for Janáček's *Jenufa*.

101. PARTISANS AND ADVERSARIES
OF JANÁČEK

We students occupied almost the entire gallery of the Old Theatre at Veveří and breathlessly watched the progress of the performance. Great was the enthusiasm. Janáček was wildly applauded and given many wreaths. After the performance he was carried on the shoulders of the soloists (as far as I remember they were still in costume) from the theatre to the Beseda House. The dramatic significance of the work was immense. From the musical point of view it made an impression of complete newness and divided us students into fervent upholders or fierce antagonists of its unusual style. We must not forget that at that time opera was judged according to the standards of Wagner which made it impossible for staunch Wagnerites to be able to stomach music so utterly opposed to Wagner in character.

Janáček was able to suggest life and truth with great spontaneity. The Wagnerites put forward the wedding march from Lohengrin as an example, which according to them, was quite above comparison with the wedding scene towards the end of Janáček's *Jenufa*. We held our own and proved to the Wagnerites that Janáček was an entirely different case and therefore entirely right.

From the memoires of Janáček's pupil, *Václav Kaprál* (1889—1947), published in the magazine, Divadelní Listy Zemského divadla v Brně, No. VII, 1931—1932, pp. 197 ff.

102. EXPLANATION OF THE CHORUS
"EVERY COUPLE..."

Dear Sir,

Allow me to explain the logic and probability of the chorus, "Every couple must endure its sorrow," in the first act of *Jenufa*. I have noticed, many times, that whoever hears it says to himself,

"Yes, after all, every couple really must endure its sorrow". Everyone feels bound to agree that the Grandmother speaks nothing but the truth. Everyone agrees with what they see on the stage. The elder has good reason to emphasize it; Laca on account of his own sufferings, repeats it; also Jenufa, with her hopeless longing, and each young man when he tells his girl of their own particular fate and mutual love: in this way the ensemble becomes more and more complicated, fills out and broadens.

But now, why are these few words repeated so often? Because I had no others at hand. But I felt that I might linger over this passage in order to give the eight-part music time to broaden out in a natural way and resolve again, naturally, into the quietest pianissimo; just as the thought fades into oblivion. Of course it is necessary for both soloists and chorus to know their parts to perfection so as to avoid having to concentrate their whole attention on the conductor's baton.

My librettist, Mrs. Preiss, offered to extend the text at this point. But it would have been of little help. It needs a more lively rendering of all three sections of the ensemble.

Why should the Grandmother, the Grandfather, Laca, Jenufa and the four-part chorus all begin with the same motive? Does not that impute the fundamental characteristic of natural melody?

First of all, I made here a slight concession on account of the music, which, had I been writing now, I would scarcely have allowed myself, in spite of the fact that the essential words of the characters and their corresponding melodic curves are here in abundance. In these curves we live with our entire spirit, and we identify ourselves with those of the stranger and suffer with him. This is the reason for the similitude covering the melody in that scene.

I am

Yours very truly,

Leoš Janáček.

To the editor of the magazine *Jeviště*, ("The Stage"), Brno, 1904.

103. NEW PRINCIPLES OF OPERA COMPOSING

In spite of the innovations which listeners to Janáček's music must encounter, the performance of *Jenufa* aroused a success such as can only have been aroused by a work which was fully understood. It resembled the success of an already known work and not at all that of an unknown opera, which also proves that the principles on which it is worked out are correct and merit further consideration.

Account of the performance of *Jenufa* taken from the magazine, *Dalibor*, No. XXVI Brno 1904, pp. 51—52.

104. THE CREATIVE RESULT IS WHAT MATTERS

For a genius to live in a small town is always unfortunate. It is difficult to say whether he suffers more from his fame at home or from being misunderstood in the world at large. The success of *Jenufa* in Brno was certainly very great, and it would be wrong to underestimate what this success meant for the composer who had, more or less, lost faith in himself. Many people, among them many musicians, saw and felt the excellent dramatic effect of the music, with its feeling deeply anchored in human crimes and reconciliations.

Everyone felt that a great rainbow of faith in eternal love arched over the whole work. Everything small and futile, earthly and materialistic, fell into insignificance. How long will it take before we discover that Janáček's theories on the music of speech are of secondary importance when considering the creative result as a whole. This is what will make Janáček live.

From the article by *K. Z. Klíma* entitled, *My Janáček*, which appeared in *Lidové Noviny* 27th April, 1941.

105. RETIRES FROM HIS POST AS TEACHER OF MUSIC

Dear Sir,

I am happy to know that you are in good health. I had begun to be anxious on account of your long silence.

Yesterday, the Czech Academy surprised me by awarding me 400 crowns for my work on the taking down of the melody of speech in notation. Which means that they recognize its importance.

Here, during the holidays, I want to listen to the Hanakian speech melody. I plan to stay a while in Přerov, in Prostějov, in Vyškov, and in Kroměříž. I plan also to regenerate the wonderful melody of speech in Slovakia. I will spend just a few days there in order to be able to visit you.

I was offered the post of Director of the Warsaw Conservatoire but we could not came to an agreement over my "zhalovaniyu"— salary, in Russian.

I now take life as it comes, as fate has ordained.

Now I am setting out for a few weeks stay at Hukvaldy.

This year I have also asked to be pensioned off. I am unable to cope with teaching those dreadful rudiments of music. And then, the unfairness – one teacher in the 8th class, another in the 9th class – and why should I be amongst those in the 10th class? Because their lordships from the county inspectorate take no notice of what goes on. And, after all, my life will not last even a fraction of another fifty years.

With kindest regards
I remain,
Yours sincerely,
Leoš Janáček.

A letter to the expert on folk art, *František Bartoš*, written some time after the 3rd July, 1904. — Janáček retired from the Teachers' Training Institute in Brno at the end of October 1904.

106. *JENUFA* ALTERED AND YET NOT PRODUCED

The operas of Janáček, the greatest Moravian composer, are dogged by a cruel fate such as they certainly do not deserve. His earlier opera, *Jenufa*, will not be heard this season in Brno although it was announced in the prospectuses. This detail proves the inefficiency of the committee, even if we leave unconsidered the other reasons for which this opera was turned down in the middle of the season. A composer of so rare a type and of such great originality as Janáček surely has the right to be performed, especially when it is known that he has made considerable alterations to his work which he deserves to hear and which the public, quite rightly, want to know and judge.

From the report by the music critic, *Hubert Doležil* (1876—1945), which appeared in the magazine, *Hudební Revue*, Vol. II, 1909, p. 71. Janáček made alterations in his *Jenufa* at various dates, especially in 1906, 1911 and 1916. Between 1907 and 1910 the work was left unperformed in Brno. In Prague it was refused.

107. REQUESTING PRAGUE TO PRODUCE *JENUFA*

Forced by the dreadful conditions of our theatre in Brno, for long only temporary, which excludes the performance of so important a work as Janáček's opera, *Jenufa*, and the general desire to see that work on the stage of the National Theatre in Prague, we would desire the management of that theatre to take immediate action for having the work performed. We see in *Jenufa* a work of such artistic importance as to deserve the widest possible attention throughout the country.

From a speech made at the Friends of Art Club in Brno, published in *Lidové Noviny*, 19th February, 1911.

108. FAITH IN THE SIXTY-YEAR OLD GENIUS

Dear Sir,

Allow us to join the circle of your most true and sincere and grateful admirers who, on the occasion of your 60th birthday (in spirit, not more than your 40th) wish that you may enjoy many years of healthy, satisfactory, happy and above all successful life during which your deserving, great and original work will be fully recognised... That time will come, for come it must. Let it not be too long delayed.

With most sincere regards

Dr and Mrs. Janke.

Luhačovice, 6th July, 1914.

Dr Zikmund Janke (1865—1918), ear, nose, throat and asthma specialist of Prague. Spent his summer-holidays at Luhačovice where he knew Janáček and collaborated with him on the libretto of the opera, The Excursion of Mr. Brouček to the Moon. This letter is published here for the first time (from the Janáček Archives in Brno).

109. APPRECIATION OF HIS ARTISTIC ACHIEVEMENTS

Dear Sir,

To your many congratulations ,I should like to add my small contribution. I hate your 60th birthday. I want to have you always as I used to know you. But even if time colours your hair with silver streaks and the years alter what they will, your artistic daring, verve and temperament, which was what I most admired during your youth, will never desert you. And this gives me pleasure on your 60th birthday. Well, dear Sir, I wish that you may remain young and healthy for many years.

In spirit, I place my hand affectionately in yours.

Alois Mrštík.

Diváky, 2nd July, 1914.

Dear friend,

I am also dissatisfied with the boiling and galloping way in which transparent, empty, destructive time plies on. What can we do, we cannot hold it back. Thank you for your kind words of remembrance. I am glad that once again there is a handful of us here in Moravia with whom I can live artistically.

Kindest regards.

Yours sincerely,

Leoš Janáček.

Brno, 5th July, 1914.

Between Janáček and the Mrštík brothers, *Vilém* and *Alois*, there grew up an artistic and personal friendship resulting from the spiritual relationship of these Czech artists in Moravia. — *Alois Mrštík* (1861—1925), Czech author; lived from 1889 at Diváky near Hustopeče and published, together with his brother *Vilém* (1863—1912), the well known drama *Maryša*. Alois was personally closer to Janáček, especially as he had studied with him at the Teachers' Training Institute in Brno, and had sung under him in the Brno Beseda. Proofs of the interesting friendship which existed between these two artists are set forth in *J. Racek's book: "The Mrštík Brothers and Their Spiritual Leanings Towards Leoš Janáček and Vítězslav Novák"* (1940).

110. THE STRUGGLE FOR *JENUFA* IN PRAGUE

Dear Friend,

I fear that it will be impossible to pave the way for *Jenufa*. I know very well that I stand alone with my musical ideas. I am understood only with difficulty. I cannot attach myself to anyone. If you knew with what unwillingness I bind myself down to anything. And in Prague, it is not necessary to exert oneself. In Brno, I sit like a magpie on its nest. Dr Elgart is still favourably inclined towards my work. I know who has the decisive word, who is allowed cut into the sun and who not.

Leoš Janáček.

Brno, 28th December, 1915.

Dear Friend,

During the last few days in Prague I have been feeling as though my brain was on fire. All I want is to finish quickly what has taken so long to prepare. I have a feeling that the first performance of *Jenufa* will come to be regarded as a memorable day. The little stone which your wife aimed with such dexterity, is bringing down with it an avalanche of prejudices and I am now able to breath more freely. My most sincere thanks. And you? You took so much trouble that certain people must have been thoroughly riled. To disturb complacent sleepers makes one unpopular. All good wishes for the New Year.

With kindest regards,
Yours sincerely,

Leoš Janáček.

Brno, 31th December, 1915.

This letter to *Dr František Veselý* is from an article which his wife, *Marie Calma-Veselý,* published in the magazine, *Listy Hudební Matice,* Prague, Vol. IV. 1925—1926. — *Dr Jaroslav Elgart,* former Medical Superintendent of the Kroměříž Hospital, Janáček's admirer. — Dr Veselý built up and was director of the Luhačovice Spa. He and his wife, Marie (born 1883), who was a writer and singer, played an important part in bringing about the production of *Jenufa* in Prague.

III. CHANGES SUGGESTED BY KAREL KOVAŘOVIC

Dear Sir,

Yesterday evening I sang through some of the songs of Jenufa and "Kostelnička". Kovařovic was very satisfied. One or two places especially pleased him. He has, however some suggestions to make, less as a composer than as an experienced theatre man. They are details. He would insert them into the piano score (he asked for a copy) and then send them to me in about a fortnight. If you agree to these small changes—I repeat, they concern the production more

13. Leoš Janáček with some of his pupils at Brno. *Sitting, from left to right:* Dr Ludvík Kundera, the present Rector of the Janáček Academy of Music and Art in Brno, Leoš Janáček, František Neumann, Chief Conductor of the Brno National Theatre (died 1929). *Standing, from left to right:* Prof. Vilém Petrželka, Břetislav Bakala, Chief Conductor of the Brno Broadcasting Orchestra, Prof. Jaroslav Kvapil, Prof. Václav Kaprál (died 1947).

14. František Neumann, (1874—1929), conductor of most of Janáček's operas
(A drawing by Eduard Milén).

than the music and some cuts, especially, in the part of Laca — he would certainly perform *Jenufa* in the spring. Kovařovic is certain that his suggestions will not harm the work. After all, Dvořák allowed him to alter *Dimitrij* and *The Jacobin*. One thing is certain, he likes *Jenufa* and, after yesterday evening, certainly likes it more. You may be sure that he would rehearse it thoroughly and see that it was well put on. He wants me to sing Jenufa. He said that no one would do it so well. The others have what he calls "brittle" voices. Horvát would sing "Kostelnička", Schütz—Števa. All that remains is for you, dear Sir, to win over Kovařovic completely for *Jenufa* by showing your good will. Kovařovic has promised me definitely that if you will agree to carry out these minor modifications, the first performance will be at the beginning of April. Within a fortnight I will send the piano score, then the best thing would be if you could manage to come to Prague, and either meet Kovařovic at our house or at the theatre. That is, of course, presuming that you will have agreed to make the alterations. Meetings are unnecessary and it will be enough if you make the changes and send the score here. Kovařovic would have it copied out by his own people. Are you satisfied ? I hope so. Kindest regards to yourself and to your wife.

Marie Calma-Veselý.

Karlín, 9th December 1915.

Janáček made some of the alterations which Kovařovic suggested. At the first performance of *Jenufa* in Prague (26th May 1916) the part of Jenufa was sung by Kamila Unger, "Kostelnička", Gabriela Horvát. Theodor Schütz, who had been suggested for the part of Števa, sang Laca.

112. OBSTACLES OVERCOME

Dear Friend,

I would like to add to my wife's letter by stating my pleasure at what has been achieved. If there had always been such friendship between you and Kovařovic, at least fifty or a hundred performances of *Jenufa* would, by now, have taken place in the National Theatre. Kovařovic fully admits the beauty and also the originality of the music; but, as a man of the theatre, he advises certain changes "to give the work even greater dramatic momentum". The cutting out of a few bars will not deprive *Jenufa* of any of its original charm, and will increase its theatrical possibilities, as Chvála also pointed out. Producers have always made alterations even in works by such people as Schiller and others. It is a common practice. In short, I am certain that you will agree to Kovařovic's alterations, and will write your next opera for the National Theatre from an entirely theatrical point of view, which would mean another première in two or three years' time. You would go far to find a better librettist than Šípek. It is a thousand pities that ten years had to pass before a reconciliation was brought about between you and Kovařovic. How much it might have meant not only for art but also for the box-office. Fügner's slogan "neither profit nor glory" should be changed by the nation to "both profit and glory"!

Kindest regards to your wife.

Your devoted friend,

Veselý.

Karlín, 9th December, 1915.

A letter from *Dr František Veselý* to Janáček. — *Emanuel Chvála* (1851—1924), Czech music critic and composer. — *Karel Šípek* (1857—1923), Czech librettist. — *Jindřich Fügner* (1822—1865), the founder of the *Sokol* movement.

113. AGREEMENT REACHED

Dear Friend,

I have already torn up two letters—that is what happens when one makes mistakes and commits stupidities out of sheer joy. I would like to thank your wife—but my head is too full and I cannot think of a single word. I am like a prisoner to whom the gate to life and freedom has opened. Can he speak? I will now write to Mr. Kovařovic to tell him to make any cuts which he sees fit. I accept everything with gratitude and will come at once to Prague. Looking forward to seeing you soon,

Kindest regards to you and your wife,

Leoš Janáček.

10th December, 1915.

Janáček's letter to *Dr František Veselý* — from the article by *Maria Calma-Veselý: The Fight for Janáček's Jenufa* published in the magazine, *Listy Hudební Matice*, Vol. IV, 1925—1926, p. 45.

114. SUCCESS AT LAST

Kunc and I have agreed that Kovařovic's alterations improve Janáček's *Jenufa*. Janáček himself has admitted as much, and, in Kunc's words: "altered certain doubtful places in the declamation, thereby accepting his pupil's criticism, published in the 'Lidové Noviny'." However, Kunc should have reproached Kovařovic, as we do, for not having performed this work sooner. In his original essay on Janáček which appeared in the "Hudební revue", 1911, Kunc wrote of Janáček's willingness to reconsider any shortcomings which might appear in *Jenufa*, but Kovařovic remained adamant and refused to recognize the opera as a new milestone in Czech operatic work. He let Janáček wait twelve years and it was not until many people, especially the Veselýs, had intervened, that *Jenufa* was at last put on, excellently produced at the National Theatre in Prague in May 1916. The high standard insisted upon and the care which Kovařovic lavished on the production and devoted to the rehearsing of the work, assured its success both at home and abroad and made up for his earlier neglect of Janáček's opera.

From my article on Janáček and Kunc which appeared in the magazine, *Rytmus* Vol. IV, 1942-1943, pp. 90-94. — *Jan Kunc* wrote detailed reviews of *Jenufa* in *Lidové Noviny*, 31st January, and 9th February 1911.

115. MAGNIFICENT REHEARSAL

Today my head is again in a whirl. The orchestral rehearsal was magnificent. "As though death had peeped in on us"—you know the place where shivers run down your spine—they played so well that it gave me quite a turn. Everything will be pure and consistent from the point of view of style.

From a letter written by Janáček to his wife in Brno, 13th May 1916. The words, *as though death had peeped in on us*, are the end of the Kostelnička's song in the Second Act.

116. JANÁČEK'S HAPPIEST DAY

Whatever the reasons for Kovařovic's original refusal to accept *Jenufa* for production, it is certain that he was the cause of one of Janáček's happiest days. Janáček admitted this in a letter to Mrs. Adéla Koudela, chairman of the "Vesna" Society in Brno.

Dear Madam,

Mindful of the fact that it was yourself and the Vesna Society, who, in the most critical days of my life, did not forget me, I take the liberty of inviting you to what will be one of my happiest days, the first performance of "Jenufa" in Prague —25th of this month.

Respectfully yours,   *Leoš Janáček.*
Brno, 16th May 1916.

117. THE ICE BREAKS

At the Prague première of *Jenufa*, on the 26th May, 1916, when Janáček was already 62 years old, he had his first great success. All the sufferings, insults and humiliations which he had experienced were then fully atoned for by his tremendous happiness. The recognition of *Jenufa* paved the way for Janáček's music which thus gained nation-wide and world-wide importance.

Mrs. *Adéla Koudela* (1858—1946), for many years chairman of the women's educational society, *Vesna*, in Brno, was a close friend of Janáček's. The first night of Jenufa was the 26th and not the 25th of May, 1916.

118. AN OPEN ROAD

Dear Sir,

Your *Jenufa* made a tremendous impression on me. I have seldom left the theatre in such a state of excitement as after Friday's performance. You hold your audience for the entire evening in a pincer-like grip. During the last few days, I have carried your work about with me in my head. I repeat to myself individual scenes, look over the pages of the score, in short I am yours, heart and soul. Your tremendous success and the high standard of performance, gave me the greatest pleasure. It was in truth the duty of the theatre to devote all its strength to right your wrongs. Accept, Sir, my sincere congratulations on your most deserved success and my wishes that now there will be an open road for your works which will surely lead to the hearts of the people.

Yours,

Ostrčil.

Smíchov, 28th May, 1916.

Otakar Ostrčil (1879—1935), Czech composer, director of the opera of the National Theatre in Prague from 1920.

119. HIS BELOVED PRAGUE

Dear Sir,

I have felt drawn towards you since the time of The *70,000* when you so sincerely congratulated me. I value your words above all else, particularly I value in you your sensitive spirit and sincerity as a composer, and would seek no better friendship than yours. Your letter gave me the greatest pleasure. I would shout it out from the housetops, were it not meant only for me.

With kindest regards, I shall always look forward to seeing you when visiting my beloved Prague.

Yours ever,

Brno, 31st May, 1916. *Leoš Janáček.*

A reply to Ostrčil's letter of the 28th May, 1916. — The *70,000* was a work for male-voice choir which Janáček wrote to words by Petr Bezruč. The first performance was given by the Prague Teacher's choir (4th May, 1914), at which Janáček was present.

120. FAITH IN HIS ARTISTIC MISSION

Dear friend,

You cannot imagine what pleasure your letter gave me. I feel as though I were living in a fairy-tale. I compose and compose, as though something were urging me on. I no longer saw any worth in my work, and scarcely believed what I said. I had become convinced that no one would ever notice anything of mine. I was quite down—my pupils had begun to advise me how to compose, and how to orchestrate. I laughed at it all, nothing else remained to me. I now feel that my life is beginning to have some purpose, and I believe in my mission. You have given me strength. Thank you most sincerely. I wish you all the best.

Your devoted,

Leoš Janáček.

Brno, 24th June 1916.

To *Josef Bohuslav Foerster.* — This letter gives proof of the wonderful way in which Janáček was strengthened in spirit by the performance of *Jenufa* in Prague, 1916. Foerster placed the letter at my disposal together with some of his other correspondence with Janáček. — The Czech composer, *Josef Bohuslav Foerster* (1859—1951) was, at that time, active in the new Vienna Conservatoire while his wife Berta Lauterer had been engaged to sing at the Court Opera, a post which she held until 1913. From 1885 Foerster was an intimate friend of Janáček and wrote criticisms of the operas produced at the National Theatre in his magazine, *Hudební Listy*. This friendship deepened after World War I, when Foerster returned to Prague.

121. *JENUFA* AS A FOLK OPERA

The music of *Jenufa*, though strongly tinctured with the folk spirit, is, in substance, a strikingly original creation. Janáček makes use of a style of melodic recitative which is said to be specifically Slovak-Moravian in rhythm and accent. What really matters for us foreigners is that—as in the case of Mussorgsky's unmistakably Russian melodic recitative—it is a method of expression admirably adapted to the utterance of varied and poignant emotion. The vocal phrases, whether they follow each other continuously or are broken by pregnant pauses, whether they are urgent with elemental passion or languid with sorrow, tense or all but quiescent, seem perfectly natural in effect. The disadvantage of the strongly localised accent and lilt need trouble only the unfortunate translators of the text. The orchestration has a colour and tang of its own. It owes nothing to the Russian or any other school of instrumentation. Sometimes there are effects which consciously aim at the imitation of local instruments used by the people—such as the "dudy", —a small bag-pipe; the "fujara"—pastoral flute; or the cymbalom: but the chief object of Janáček's orchestration is to enforce, and comment upon, psychological situations, not to paint tone pictures.

From Rosa Newmarch's essay: *Leoš Janáček and Moravian Music Drama*, published in *The Slavonic Revue*, 1922—1923.

122. UNFAVORABLE CRITICISM OF *JENUFA*

It must be stated, quite openly, that his works are unsatisfactory, not only from the artistic but also from the ethnographical point of view. When we consider the life of the Moravian people, we get a more subtle, organic and altogether more probable picture than is provided by the old ethnographical school of thought to which Leoš Janáček belongs. The greater, therefore, are our objections from the artistic point of view. Here, the old truth has been proved anew, that life cannot be pieced together, but can only be created. Janáček, it is true, collects sufficient material but is unable to make anything of it. Leaving aside his unending repetition of certain words which, in some places, culminates in unintentional comedy, we can best see where Janáček's primitivism leads by observing his artificial form. Janáček even tries to write duets, naturally not polyphonic, but only melodic, as though in real life people interrupted each other. The impossibility and lifelessness of Janáček's style is most obvious in his choral works and peasant scenes. It is here that we should expect the fullest life, at least in the ethnographical sense, but it is just here that the composer leaves us most cold . . . Even *Jenufa* is an old "Singspiel" in a new cloak and it bears within it all the evils of that type of work, to which Smetana opposes his highly cultured art.

From a review of Janáček's work by *Zdeněk Nejedlý* (1878—) Czech musicologist, author of a number of scholarly works on Smetana and a vast history of Hussite songs. Nejedlý's criticism was published in the magazine, *Smetana*, Vol. VI, 1916, No. 9—10, August 4th.

123. IN DEFENCE OF *JENUFA*

A detailed article on Janáček's *Jenufa* has appeared in the magazine *Smetana*, No. 9—10, Vol. VI. This article, with its completely negative attitude, was an isolated instance in the general approbation shown for the work. The success was manifested not only in the theatre but also among the critics. We consider *Jenůfa* to be a work of great importance and a rich gift to the nation, especially precious on account of its having been produced in these days. We are pleased to observe that the public have probably been made aware of the worth of Janáček's works and will now be able to experience to the full the extreme pleasure which they are capable of giving. By good fortune it is at this moment that they may get to know a work, which, although differently, reaches to the same depths in the feelings of our people as do those of Smetana, and in which they will find very many moments of pure and new artistic expression drawn from what today forms our strongest inner support. Music can achieve more in these hard times than to become the subject of enthusiasm, or of criticism, always shallow, however well meant, or what may even be damaging, violent refutation for the sake of some dry dogma, partiality or prejudice. Here we have proof: it has, in fact, produced devotion and love.

If the author of this article was convinced that the recruiting scene in Janáček's work does not contain real gaiety and is cold, I, myself, see in it a splendid embodiment of Moravian passion, easily fired and capable of anything. It is a complete picture of male brutality, yet astonishingly Slavonic in its languid intoxication from which there is only one step to tragedy. It would be a fundamental mistake to imagine that Janáček patches together the melodic lines of *Jenůfa* from bits of folk music gathered in Moravia and only adds his own where his collection is insufficient. If this were so, then we should really be dealing with gross naturalism which supposes naively that "real, natural forms as life presents them can be carried over into art".

If someone were to ask me to classify in one word Janáček's works, I would perhaps say realism; that is, a style distinguished from naturalism only by its lighter, finer shading, and not fundamentally.

If I were certain of being properly understood, then I would not be afraid to say naturalism. The masters of naturalism have given us many a *chef d'ouevre*, while those who only professed naturalism without possessing true artistic greatness, have produced nothing but mediocrities. The same applies to idealism, as not even the most idealistic attitude is protection against mediocrity if the artist himself is not sufficiently outstanding. So it always was, is, and will be.

Dr Václav Štěpán (1889—1944) composer, pianist and music critic wrote an essay on *Jenufa* which appeared in the magazine, *Hudební revue*, Vol. X, 1916—1917, pp. 28—40 and from which the above excerpt is taken. It was written in answer to Prof. Zdeněk Nejedlý's criticism of Janáček's *Jenufa*.

124. NO FOLK SONGS IN JENUFA

Dear Sir,

Your words breathe forth friendship. I am sorry that there was no opportunity of talking to you for a longer time in that spirit. I make haste to thank you from my heart. Certainly, as soon as I come to Prague to hear *Jenufa*, I will look you up. In answer to one of your remarks, let me assure you that there is not a single foreign or folk melody in *Jenufa*. Even the recruiting song and the wedding song, except for the text, are my own. Do not be offended that I make such a point of it; this mistake was made by the paper *Venkov* and, in the audience, the public made similar remarks about it. So long, then. Let us make it a happy occasion.

Yours sincerely,

Leoš Janáček.

Brno, 30th May 1916.

Janáček's letter to *Dr V. Štěpán*. This letter explains the question of the melody in the recruiting song in the first act and of the wedding song in the third act, both of which were wrongly considered to be folk songs.

125. MAX BROD POINTS OUT JOSEF SUK TO JANÁČEK

Dear Friend,

I well remember the dress rehearsal of *Jenufa*. I know that it was you who were pointed out to me by Dr Max Brod and so making one of those links in the chain of events. It is my wish that you may also find such an advocate who sees as deeply into your spirit as Brod sees into mine.

Leoš Janáček.

From a letter written to *Josef Suk* from Hukvaldy, 6th July, 1924. From the book by *J. M. Květ: "Living words of Josef Suk"*, Prague, 1946.

126. MAX BROD TO JANÁČEK

Dear Sir,

My words are too weak to express my admiration for your genius. I am glad, however, that my insufficient description caused you some pleasure.

I should be very honoured if you would visit me on Sunday next at my house in Prague V., Břehová 8. I shall be at home the whole morning and in the afternoon until six o'clock.

I esteem in you not only the great musician, but also your heroic moral principles, which make you stride through life without compromise and without looking either to left or to right.

Yours very respectfully,

Max Brod.

Prague, 28th November, 1916.

Max Brod was made aware by the composer *Josef Suk* (1875—1935) of Janáček's *Jenufa* and did important work in forwarding not only this opera, but all Janáček's compositions in Austria and in Germany. Later Janáček called him in gratitude *a messenger of Heaven.* — In this letter addressed to Leoš Janáček, Max Brod responds to the composer's thanks for his essay on *Jenufa*, published in the magazine, *Berliner Schaubühne*, 16th November, 1916, under the title, *Tschechisches Operngl ck.* The importance of Brod is clearly demonstrated in the book, *The Correspondence of Max Brod and Leoš Janáček*, Prague, 1953, edited by *Jan Racek* and *Artuš Rektorys.*

127. *JENUFA* IN VIENNA

Today was a dress rehersal at the Vienna Court Opera. The setting was exactly as it will be on the first night. What exquisite colour—150 costumes—what a wonderfully large stage and everything new and shining! The mill with the beautiful highlands in the background. Sun-flooded—it will certainly make the public perspire. The recruits with the mill-hand on a garlanded horse— yes, I was longing for such a production in Prague, in vain.

Mrs. Weidt acts wonderfully—coached by the producer. She is a soprano and therefore has not got your dark, silken voice that fits so well to the part—but she acts perfectly. You must see it. At certain moments it really gives you the shivers. And how well imagined—Jenufa is ideal. How these two women compete! There are no words to describe it. The director Gregor told Mrs. Weidt that she is singing a part such as she has never known or sung in her life. The rehearsal went off well. Tomorrow there will be another run through, just to freshen up their memories, and the day after tomorrow is the full dress-rehearsal. The Bohemian Quartet is passing through Vienna tomorrow and they asked to be allowed to attend it. The reporters are after me and every day the local press is full of *Jenufa*...

From Janáček's letter to *Gabriela Horvát*, an outstanding "Kostelnička" at the National Theatre in Prague. The letter was written from Vienna on the 12th February, 1918, before the Vienna premiere of *Jenufa* (16th February, 1918). Jenufa was sung by Maria Jeritza (1891) "Kostelnička" by Mrs. Weidt. — *Hans Gregor* was the director of the Vienna Court Opera from 1911 to 1918. — *The Bohemian Quartet* comprised Karel Hoffmann, Josef Suk, Jiří Herold and Ladislav Zelenka, of whom the only living member today (1955) is Ladislav Zelenka.

128. A VOCIFEROUS SUCCESS

A successful opera, brimming over with music. Many effective operas will lose their artistic value, when compared with this one, which is in fact a slice of real life. The composer had to give way to the public at the end of the second and third acts, because of the storms of applause, and appeared about twenty times on the stage alone and with the soloists.

From a review of the Vienna production of *Jenufa*, which took place on the 16th February 1918 and was conducted by Hugo Reichenberger (1873—1938). The reviews of *Jenufa* in Austria and Germany were published by the *Universal Edition* in a special circular with a portrait of Janáček and of Maria Jeritza, who sang Jenufa. The libretto was translated by Max Brod.

129. HOME AND FOREIGN PRODUCTIONS COMPARED

Since the Vienna days of old I was again once more in Vienna; and today I arrived here from Prague. There is now great jealousy between Prague and Vienna. Where is the best production? Well—it is more heart-felt in Prague. It is home; though poorer, it is nearer to the heart. Believe me, I was so worked up about everything that I am longing for quiet. Now, I have to arrange unpleasant financial problems. All sorts of people are after my money.

Does that "plant of fame" still grow? Look after it well! Fame has gone to my knees, but it hurts there. I have to take hot mud-baths, otherwise I shall start limping.

Brno, 5th March, 1918.

From Janáček's letter to his friend *Mrs. Kamila Stössel*.

130. UNHAPPINESS

You have no idea, how unhappy I am...

From a letter to *Mrs. Kamila Stössel* written on the 15th April, 1918.

131. DIFFICULTIES WITH KOVAŘOVIC'S ALTERATIONS TO *JENUFA*

You know best what it is to compose and what it is to make alterations. A pack of queer people want to put both on the same level—and make profit out of me. I simply wanted to forbid, for the future, Kovařovic's alterations, but that would have meant complications for other theatres, which is the reason why I decided to meet these people half way in this matter. I would ask you and Mr. Ostrčil to act for me as experts. Two will also be appointed from the other side. Choose the fifth yourself. I ask that the fifth should be familiar with the law. Either a judge or a lawyer. I should suggest Dr Löwenbach. I have drafted the questions myself. They may be worded differently. From my questions you can see that I am meeting Mrs. Kovařovic more than half way because I have been told that she is in need.

Kindest regards,

Yours sincerely,

Leoš Janáček.

Brno, 1st January, 1924.

TO FRANTIŠEK NEUMANN

1. Does the success of *Jenufa* on the stage depend on the alterations of Mr. Kovařovic?

2. If *Jenufa* was successfully given from 1904 to 1916 under the direction of Doubravský, Lacina, Jiříkovský and conductors such as Hrazdira and Winkler and a c c e p t e d i n t h e o r i g i n a l b y K o v a ř o v i c f o r p e r f o r m a n c e a t t h e N a t i o n a l T h e a t r e i n P r a g u e, is it necessary to make mere alterations which were not ordered and not asked of me?

3. Did these alterations come under the competence of the director of the opera and the conductor if he made them o f h i s o w n a c c o r d a n d w a s p a i d f o r t h e m b y t h e t h e a t r e m a n a g e m e n t? Does the composer have to pay

for them, though as long as Kovařovic lived, he never asked him to do so?

4. As Kovařovic made an arrangement with the theatre management, without my knowledge, for 1% royalties which he received and I, who want to help Mrs. Kovařovic purely privately and voluntarily am offering her 1% of my royalties from every production of *Jenufa* at the National theatre,—a r e   t h e s e   a l t e r-a t i o n s   s u f f i c i e n t l y   w e l l   p a i d ?

5. If, with Kovařovic's   k n o w l e d g e   and   w i t h o u t a n y   r e s e r v a t i o n s   a n d   w i t h o u t   m a k i n g   a n y d e m a n d   f o r   c o m p e n s a t i o n   from the composer or from the publisher, these alterations were printed in the score, am I obliged to pay anything to the widow of Kovařovic?

Janáček was against the unauthorised and unasked-for alterations of Karel Kovařovic to his opera *Jenufa*. He was willing to help the widow who was in need, but he defended his point of view that the widow had no right to any part of his royalties as the alterations had already been paid for by the management of the theatre during Kovařovic's life time. *František Neumann* (1874-1929), from 1919, director of the Brno opera, before that, conductor at the theatre in Frankfurt-on-Main. — *Otakar Ostrčil* succeeded Kovařovic as director of the opera in the National theatre. — *Dr Jan Löwenbach* (1880—), lawyer and writer on music, was to have intervened in the suit as an authority on copyright.

132. JANÁČEK AND PRAGUE

The star of Janáček's dramatic art rose over Prague with the production of *Jenufa* in the National Theatre on the 26th May 1916. Until that time Prague had heard, apart from the male voice choruses which had been performed by the Prague "Hlahol" society (1906), the cantata, *Our Father* (1906), *Maryčka Magdonová* to words by Petr Bezruč (1909), *70,000* (1914) and, of his orchestral works, only the overture, *Jealousy* (introduction to *Jenufa*, 1906) and the folk ballet *Rákoš Rakoczy* (1891). The overture to *Jenufa* was performed in Prague by František Neumann who, later, became an enthusiastic admirer and interpreter of Janáček's works in Brno.

After the victorious production of Jenufa in Prague under the direction of Karel Kovařovic, Prague was won over for good by Janáček's art. The first performance of the orchestral ballad *The Fiddler's Child* given by the Czech Philharmonic Orchestra conducted by Otakar Ostrčil in 1917, and the first performance of the cantata *Everlasting Gospel*, given by the Prague "Hlahol" society conducted by Jaroslav Křička (1917) were further mile-stones on the road to artistic advance and stabilisation of the operatic, symphonic and vocal works of Janáček at the end of the first World War.

From my article about Janáček's *Jenufa*, which appeared in the fortnightly magazine, *Národní Divadlo*, Vol. XVIII, 1941, No. 9, 26th February. — *Jaroslav Křička* (1882—), Czech composer and conductor.

133. LONGING FOR PRAGUE

I simply must go to "golden" Prague. I feel like part of the clock's mechanism; it has sense as long as it is in the clock. Pull it out and it becomes useless. If I had to stay in Brno I should become as useless as the part which has been taken out. I am well aware of this and therefore I am so often out of sorts.

From Janáček's letter to his friend, *Mrs. Kamila Stössel*, 28th June, 1918.

134. ARTISTIC DEVELOPMENT IN MORAVIA

I have one great joy: Moravia alone is enough to give me all necessary inspiration. So rich are its sources.

Brno, 9th of June 1916.

From Janáček's letter to the National Theatre Association in Brno. It was first published by *Firkušný* in the magazine *Musicology*, Vol. I, 1938. — *Leoš Firkušný* (1905—1950), author o f many essays on Janáček

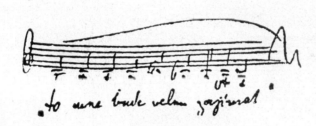

15. Janáček's transcriptions of the melodic curves of speech.

16. Leoš Janáček with the violin teacher Otakar Ševčík (left) and a pupil (centre).

135. IN MEMORY OF AN ASSASINATED WORKER

The call for the establishment of a Czech University in Brno was in vain. The Brno Germans instigated a spirit of antagonism to everything Czech. And in the so-called *Volkstag*, that is to say, the parliament of all Germans from former Austria, on the 1st October, 1905, they proclaimed that they would never agree to the establishment of a Czech University in Brno. There were street clashes between demonstrators of both camps which often led to bloodshed. The Beseda house in Brno became a centre and refuge of the Czechs. On that fateful second of October, when the army was called out to intervene, the Czech demonstrators had left the Beseda house singing patriotic songs. The German squad fell upon a young joiner's mate, František Pavlík, at the gate of the Beseda house and one of the soldiers drove his bayonet into the unarmed, twenty-year-old workman. Pavlík was taken to hospital where he died. A few months later another young workman, František Rezel, also fell a victim to the street clashes.

Janáček was the only artist in Brno to react by producing a work, influenced by the death of Pavlík: a piano sonata in three movements: *Foreboding, Death* and *Death March*, which he entitled *1. X. 1905*, in protest against the use of force. During rehearsal, however, he was prompted by his severe self-criticism to scrap the last section of the cycle which he threw into the fire. The two remaining sections prove Janáček's strong social leanings which are also apparent in his cantata, *Our Father*, his settings of Bezruč's verse, his symphonic ballad *The Fiddler's Child* and his opera, *The House of the Dead*. In his work *1. X. 1905*, Janáček openly showed his fervent interest in the Czech University in Brno and joined the ranks of those fighting for its establishment. When, at last, in 1928 the Czech University of Brno was formally given the name of the first president of the Czechoslovak Republic, T. G. Masaryk, Janáček dedicated his *Festival Chorus* to the newly-founded University, and proudly accepted an honorary doctorate.

From my preface to Janáček's piano sonata *1. X. 1905*.

The white marble staircase
Of the Beseda house in Brno...
Indelibly stained with the blood of the simple workman František
Pavlík —
He came to demonstrate for a University
And was bayoneted by cruel murderers.

Leoš Janáček.

In memory of a worker stabbed to death during a manifestation
for the University of Brno.

From the title-page of the piano sonata entitled *Street Scene—1. X. 1905.*

136. WITH PETR BEZRUČ AGAINST SOCIAL AND NATIONAL OPPRESSION

It is interesting to note that Janáček began setting words by the poet, Petr Bezruč, immediately after the demonstrations and street clashes in Brno to which the young Czech workman, Pavlík fell a victim (1905). The first of Bezruč's works to be set by Janáček was *Kantor Halfar*, perhaps because it concerned the life of a poor schoolmaster, a subject which was very dear to Janáček—the schoolmaster's son. The main reason for his finding Bezruč's material sympathetic was his strong aversion for the mighty of this world, an unwillingness to submit and faith in the national idea. Janáček, the sincere patriot and protector of the poor and the oppressed, found in the school-master, Halfar, a model of proud resistance.

Janáček succeeded in catching the psychological atmosphere of Bezruč's ballad in his music. With Janáček the psychology is always that of the collective, that is to say, he is never satisfied with his personal conceptions of the idea but asks himself what might be the attitude of the collective body or even of all humanity. From this source springs Janáček's repetition of musical phrases which he considered to be not only the psychological echo of words and themes in thoughts but also their further impact on the collective, that is, a complete mood and its reflection in sound. A good example of this is the moment where the school-master is found hanged on the apple tree. The first and second tenor repeat the words after each other twice in imitation while the first and second bass repeat four times the single word, "school-master", in the form of a question. This is the frame work of Janáček's creative method when using voices for the words of Petr Bezruč. He constructs a collective drama of people, which has deep psychological foundations and which he divides up into several groups of voices to complete the whole dramatic situation. From here also come Janáček's methods of working on the text. He goes so far as to suggest thoughts in music—"Is it the school master?" He anticipates the words of coming verses and, for psychological reasons, repeats the words concerning what has already happened. In short, he completes the actions and thoughts and feelings of the whole collective. In his *Kantor Halfar*, Janáček was trying out methods which he later succeeded in carrying on into his works, *Maryčka Magdonová* and the *70,000*. The form of *Kantor Halfar* is a rondo, with imitations and variations. Melodically it grows almost entirely from one theme, the simple harmonies of which are enriched with sustained pedal notes. Short themes in lively rhythm, disturbing the otherwise smooth surface of the music, are carried over from his orchestral style into his choral works. The alternating melodies and harmonies sharpen or soften Janáček's dramatic situations. The half epical, half lyrical spirit interweaves with sharp drama. Among the characteristic traits of the central figures, the school-master's firmness and refusal to give in, the inspector's cruelty and the hardness of those in authority, stand out. All this is very sharply portrayed in Janáček's stylisation. The ending, in which the music describes how the school-master was allotted a corner of the churchyard, rings out in dumb reconciliation.

Janáček's *Halfar*, for male-voice choir is a setting of words by Petr Bezruč (1867), author of *Songs of Silesia* (1906). — From my essay which appeared in the *Silesian Anthology*, (Opava 1953).

137. *MARYČKA MAGDONOVÁ* FOR MALE VOICE CHOIR

I was most agreeably surprised, yesterday, to receive your splendid choral work *Maryčka Magdonová*, especially the dedication which strengthens our old friendship. I send you my most heartfelt and sincere thanks.

I wish you from my heart that all your future works may be as successful and as popular as is your very beautiful and rousing *Maryčka Magdonová*.

From a letter written on the 1st October (1909) by *Ferdinand Vach*, who performed, with great success, Janáček's choral works at a time when *Jenufa* had still not been accepted for performance in Prague. *Maryčka Magdonová* was first performed on the 20th April (1908) and first published in 1909.

138. JANÁČEK AND VACH

I first met Janáček in the year 1893 in Brno during a meeting of music teachers at the Teaching Institute. The meeting had been called by Janáček. I was the chairman. For me the meeting was important in that it marked the beginning of my friendship with Janáček.

I came to know Janáček not only as a composer of great individuality, but as a strong character who knew how to hold his own against waverers. At that time I was active in Kroměříž, where I performed *Amarus* with success, for the first time, although the performance was not of a very high standard on account of the insufficient numbers of the county orchestra. When, in 1903, I founded the Moravian Teacher's choir (young teachers from the Kroměříž Institute), Janáček was not interested in this new choir until he had heard us perform this work in 1904 at, as far as I remember, Veselí-on-Morava. He was very surprised and immediately sent me an interesting letter and two further choral works, *Dež víš* and *Klekanica*. Having looked through these works I recognized them as of real value, and this I immediately told the composer, and straight away, sent the parts to be copied.

In 1907 he sent me *Maryčka Magdonová*. He played it to me on the piano. I took an immediate fancy to it, but I was afraid to perform it. I would have considered it too "new" even for the Teacher's chorus, and I was not wrong. It was not only a question of intonation, rhythm and dynamics, but of something more. Many rehearsals were necessary, tiring rehearsals, and even then we were afraid that it was too difficult for us. We were being worn out by exhausting work when, in 1908, we found ourselves with a concert in Paris. We put forward all our strength and gave the first performance of "Maryčka" in Prostějov where the composer was present. The success was great, but only from certain quarters. After the concert the local deputy, Eduard Skála, told the composer confidentially: "Your *Maryčka* is a socialist rally." Janáček calmly replied: "That was what I had intended." After that *Maryčka* was given in Paris. It would not be fair to speak of lack of success — it was successful, but in a Parisian way; after the concert the audience rushed out of the hall and plunged into the delights of the capital. *Maryčka Magdonová* gained a far more spontaneous success in Prague. Although our opinions were sometimes divided, it is nevertheless my pride that I also contributed towards removing prejudices against a work which long remained unrecognised.

From the article by *Ferdinand Vach* which appeared in the magazine *Hudební Rozhledy*, Vol. 1, 1924—1925 pp. 38—39, entitled *Reminiscences*. — Janáček dedicated his settings of Bezruč's *Kantor Halfar* and *Maryčka Magdonová* to Vach. — The Moravian Teacher's choir gave the first performance of *Amarus* in Kroměříž in 1900.

139. HIS DEMANDS ON VOCAL REPRODUCTION

Janáček's *Maryčka Magdonová* was the great attraction on the programme. The composer here shows himself to be a bold realist, an Uprka in the music of Moravian Slovakia. Janáček combines folklore and naturalism with the great artistic technique of modern music. His harmonies are rugged and hard as the Moravian people. The words of the chorus pulsate with life. To this is added polyphony which outdoes the notorious modern counterpoint of Reger. The only objection to this unusual type of art is that it surpasses the possibilities of a male choir and demands of the human voice what would be more suitable for musical instruments. The moment when *Maryčka Magdonová* plunges into the river Ostravice, the music becomes more instrumental than vocal. That is why it does not ring with the usual smoothness of a male-voice choir.

From the review by *Jan Branberger* (1877—1952), music critic and later professor of the State Conservatoire in Prague, which appeared in the paper *Čas*, No. 22, 3rd December 1909. Janáček was not familiar with counterpoint as used by Reger in his polyphonic style.

140. *MARYČKA*—TRAGEDY OF THE MINING PEOPLE

Maryčka Magdonová is the result of Janáček's studies in human speech... which is the reason why his music is, and indeed can not be otherwise than entirely Czech, a quintessence of local, native voices. Janáček, as a pupil of Křížkovský, outdid his master — one might almost say, stands on his shoulders. In regard to melody, however, he should have come back to him. The tunes which we remember at one hearing and whistle when we leave the theatre, are not usually the worst. When I say we—I mean the public. It is as though the composer had given us a bit of himself. I have a feeling that I know where Janáček falls short. He had not yet composed for a sufficient length of time, he had not yet unfolded sufficiently nor had he found his true inspiration. He was hemmed in by cramping conditions like a bird in a cage. He was like a large fish floundering about in a brook and bruising himself against the stones for lack of water...

Janáček conceived *Maryčka Magdonová* as a collective dramatic scene whose overture consists of a few introductory verses about the parents and whose epilogue describes the tragic churchyard. The culminating scene is by the river, showing where the dead girl from the mountains lies. This scene is narrated, musically, in a wonderful way. Breathless flies the song and breathless we listen to the cries, tears and to the whole story of *Maryčka Magdonová*. We have relived the tragedy of a miner's daughter from Těšín. Our hearts contract and the blood hammers in our temples and long after the song has ceased, we still hear, throbbing within us, the main scene of the entire poem, the despairing tone ringing from the Těšín region, the voice of a down-trodden people. Only Leoš Janáček is capable of producing a tone poem of this kind.

From an article by *Jan Herben* (1857—1936), Czech writer, which appeared in the paper Čas, Vol. XXII, No. 207, 29th July, 1908.

141. JANÁČEK HAS TO BE SUNG

Maryčka is a new proof of Janáček's determined struggle for faithful artistic interpretation and for the final expression achieved in the second version (C sharp minor) written about the 21st March, 1907. If it is true that the first version of *Maryčka*, December 1906, was the result of ouside inspiration from the melodrama of that name by Karel Moor (1873—1945), which did not satisfy Janáček, the second version, on the contrary, had all the signs of his social revolt and his hard-hitting spirit. Janáček made use of Bezruč's aphoristic way of thinking—not unlike his own—with penetrating understanding. First of all he prepared for *Maryčka Magdonová* by a direct experience of his own. He was determined to study the sound chaos in Vítkovice, Ostrava, and Staré Hamry, to come into contact with miners and to get to know their speech melodies. He even considered an orchestral version of *Maryčka* but finally decided to leave it as a male-voice choir. He drew from his instrumental style, the typical short motives which increases the dramatic tension. This style grew out of Janáček's lively dislike for the German character of music; that is, on the one hand, against the counterpoint and the Wagnerian Leitmotiv and, on the other hand, against dramatic ostentation, pomposity and formalism. When setting Bezruč's pungent verse to music, he changed and left out words, combining several verses and repeating the dramatically important verses in various voices, while the remaining voices continued with the main poem. The mixing of several verses and the repeating of the verses, vocal insertions in the form of reminiscences, past and future words, leads Janáček to achieve highly individual polymelodic and not polyphonic work, in which each voice sings its own melodic pattern with expression corresponding to the text. It is possible to object that this word and tone variety brings about chaos as regards content and music, and becomes incomprehensible, but in this Janáček shows his genius. He is able, by using various rhythms and by the balance of the various voices, to bring out the dramatic main point and to tune the choir into a single stream of strength and conviction. There is no doubt that speech and its melodic curves so determinedly followed by Janáček, formed his dramatic expression and combative utterance. This does not mean, as Jan Herben maintains, that a work rather to be recited than sung has come into being. It is a fundamental mistake to interpret Janáček in a naturalistic way and to be always looking for the speech melodies. Janáček must be sung only in a dramatic way. Therein lies the basis for the correct interpretation of his works.

From my article which appeared in the *Silesian Anthology*, Opava, 1953.

142. JANÁČEK'S CHORUS *THE 70,000*

The third and the last of Janáček's settings of Petr Bezruč's words is *The 70,000*. It came into being shortly after the great success of *Maryčka* in December, 1909. The newness and difficulty of this work is due, above all, to the way in which the voices and choir are scored. Janáček demands the alternating of a solo quartet with the rest of the choir. He takes the first solo tenor up to top C, makes solo use of the first bass, and doubles certain voices, while the choir, in contrast, is worked out in a more homophonic manner. Janáček creates an effect of dramatic tension by making the solo tenors seem to emit cries while the sobbing of the quartet gradually develops into a proud resistance and a demand for the right to live. The closing section, starting from *Presto (Give us...)* must not be regarded as a tone picture of a noisy inn, but as a general invitation to escape despair and to rise against the violator, Baron Gero. That is also why Janáček's: *Pain, pain...* rings out with devil-may-care arrogance, and rises to a final culminating *Forte*.

Bezruč's poem is a work of which every word rings out like a cry. Only a simple stylisation can here be true and really effective. Janáček's setting is all this. The style is simple, there is not a single unnecessary note which does not depend on the text, and which is only included for the sake of sound or for the special working out of motives. Everywhere there is the truthfulness about which Janáček wrote so much and which he demanded. It is again a complete drama, played not by actors but by ordinary people, dour and suffering.

Janáček's technical methods do not intrude themselves. From the melodic and rhythmic point of view, we can find here five selected themes which, while running alongside each other, also create the melodic basis of the work.

The following theme:

is most important. It appears, sometimes in quick time and sometimes in slow time, throughout the work. Janáček's three choral works to Bezruč's words are witnesses of the great struggle of two kindred artists against social and national oppression.

From the same article.

143. DIFFICULTIES WITH THE OPERA *DESTINY*

The opera *Destiny* which Janáček composed in the years 1903 and 1904, was offered to the Brno National Theatre for the autumn season of 1906. This production fell through, however, because Ludvík Čelanský had taken a copy to Prague, announcing his intention of giving the work its first performance at the Vinohrady Theatre. The score was left lying at the Vinohrady Theatre from 1907 to 1914, and Janáček was kept waiting with empty promises. In 1911 the management of the Vinohrady Theatre pledged themselves to perform the work during the season of 1912—1913, again without keeping their word. Janáček sued the theatre in order to protect his copyright. His lawyer was Dr. Pauk, but the case never came to anything.

Ludvík Vítězslav Čelanský (1870–1931), Czech conductor and composer. He was director of the opera at the Vinohrady Theatre in Prague from 1907—1909. Janáček's opera *Destiny* has not yet been performed. He had planned to make some alterations in it similar to those which he made in *Jenufa*. On the 18th September, 1934, the Brno broadcasting station gave a broadcast performance, however, under the direction of Janáček's pupil, Břetislav Bakala (1897—).

144. THE BALLAD *THE FIDDLER'S CHILD*

My dear friend,

After the excitement of Prague, I am coming to myself. I realised how important it was to perform *The Fiddler's Child*.

Your excellent rendering helped the work to success. It was not an easy task to ensure that the work held its ground in the onslaught of the other compositions in the programme.

From our first meeting, I found you sympathetic. Now I am really fond of you. You have penetrated deep into my soul, where the work also lay. It is a difficult thing to understand.

I shall be pleased if it is possible for us to meet again under similar circumstances. I have faith in you because I see how you divide your heart among each of us composers and yet, during the performance you are able to give it to each work entirely.

Please remember me to the young ladies who accompanied you and whom I had the honour of meeting during the concert.
Yours very sincerely

Leoš Janáček.

Brno, 17th November, 1917.

To *Otakar Ostrčil* after the performance of the symphonic Ballad, *The Fiddler's Child* by the Czech Philharmonic Orchestra on the 14th November 1917.

145. DEMANDING THE BEST RENDERING

Dear friend,

My sincerest thanks for your efforts. One thing, however, must be improved: the solo for the three violins. The leader must be a first-class player with a good tone. I would suggest Mr. Maixner of the National Theatre. He would certainly be willing to do it for you. Their playing must be outstanding and perfect from all points of view. I am arriving on Sunday morning. Where will you be rehearsing? I should like to suggest a few small additions to the orchestration. With kindest regards,
Yours,

Leoš Janáček.

Prague, 31st January, 1917.

To *Jaroslav Křička*, who conducted Janáček's cantata, *Everlasting Gospel* at a concert given by the Hlahol Singing Society on the 5th February, 1917.

146. AFTER A REHEARSAL OF *EVERLASTING GOSPEL*

We were sitting in a restaurant with Janáček after one of the rehearsals of his beautiful cantata *Everlasting Gospel* before its first performance.

"Do you realise, Sir, that the fourth horn plays only one note during the whole cantata?"

"Are you sure?"

"All through you have written for three horns, and not until the very last bar, is there a chord in four parts."

We expected one of the following replies, either: "It doesn't matter, let him have a rest" or: "Let us scrap that one note. It is a tutti, and will not matter." But he replied differently, unexpectedly: "Let us add something for him!"

This sentence gives proof of Janáček's well-known attitude to his finished works. He often left finishing touches for the conductor and was not particular about alterations in technique or in notes, although, at other times he could almost include a whole poem in one note.

From a letter written by *Jaroslav Křička* to the compiler of this book.

147. AGAINST THE PETTINESS OF THE BOURGEOISIE

There are as many Mr. Broučeks among the Czechs as there are Oblomovs among the Russians. I want us to be disgusted by such people, to stamp on them and strangle them when we meet them—but, most important of all, to destroy them in ourselves. Then we shall be regenerated in the divine steadfastness of our national heroes. We must not let Mr. Brouček spoil things for us as Oblomov did for the others. A great day is approaching . Will the shadows of doubt, weakness, unbelief and subjection be smoothed away from our brows? Will the star of hope shine forth? These thoughts were the firing impulse to work; the worse the time, the quicker the avalanche of ideas for composition. It is time for the work to be brought to life. It is time for it to speak! Such thoughts as these kept my pen to the paper when I was writting *The Excursions of Mr. Brouček*. The story is from Svatopluk Čech; Mašek adds his thoughts; Holý, some variations; Dr. Janke, his additions; Gellner intervenes with humour, Mahen remains the master of the whole; Viktor Dyk carves the motto; František Procházka makes the songs. If I wanted to joke, I might ask in the words of the folk song:

> Wait, let us see
> let us count,
> if no one is missing.

Is it an exceptional, unprecedented, joint work? On the contrary. Only small seeds were sown. The point was to make them grow and blossom.

Taken from Janáček's article, *The Excursions of Mr. Brouček to the Moon and to the XVth Century*, which appeared in *Lidové Noviny*, 23rd December 1917. — *Karel Mašek* (1868—1922), Czech author and playwright (pseudonym, *Fa Presto*), wrote several successful librettos. — *Josef Holý* (1874—1928), Czech poet. — *Dr Zikmund Janke* (1865—1918), Editor; well known as a doctor at the Spa of Luhačovice. — *František Gellner* (1881—1914), Czech writer. — *Svatopluk Čech* (1846—1908), one of the greatest Czech poets. — *Jiří Mahen* (1882—1939), Czech author and playwright. *Viktor Dyk* (1877—1931), Czech poet. — *František S. Procházka* (1861—1939), Czech short-story writer. Compare, *The Correspondence of Leoš Janáček with the Librettists of the Excursions of Mr. Brouček*, Prague 1950.

148. MISUNDERSTANDING WITH MAHEN

Dear Sir,

I have found out to my amazement that you have also let my friend, Mr. Dyk, write the libretto for Mr. Brouček. I request an explanation. When and where.

Jiří Mahen.

8th September, 1916.

Dear Friend,

Why with amazement?

How could I throw away my work; work which has taken me three years? In my principles of composition, in which the words suggest the melodies, the entire melody is dependent on the sentence, it is not otherwise possible. I am not one of those composers who can fit any text to their melodies.

I began work on the first sentence,—and realised that I could not do it. On Friday, after reading through your draft, I realised that with the best will in the world, I would be unable to use it. Not because I found there any superficiality, but because I would have to rewrite everything.

I would be very glad if you could visit me and then I would be able to make quite clear to you the impossibility of reworking it a second time.

Mr. Viktor Dyk approved of the original text. He did not alter anything, except for the ending which he changed so as to keep exactly to the original of Svatopluk Čech, where the ending takes place in the apartment of Mr. Brouček.

Mr. Dyk is also never mentioned as the librettist.

I would be much obliged to you if we could meet so that I might clearly persuade you that I do not interfere with your work with any bad intentions but that although I found your work excellent, I cannot use it as it differs too much from the original and I would be unable to use a single note of what I have written.

Yours very sincerely,

Leoš Janáček.

Brno, 13th September, 1916.

Jiří Mahen justified Janáček's right to adapt the libretto without interference.

149. ACKNOWLEDGEMENT OF THE ANALYSIS OF THE OPERA *EXCURSIONS OF MR. BROUČEK*

You have written it very well; concisely, fluently. You have pointed out the action and aptly drawn attention to the themes. What a number! I would never have thought that there were so many. I know very well that the melodic material, in my work changes according to the circumstances under which it is used. You have succeeded excellently, in understanding the relationship of the themes to each other. They must grow one out of another, they cannot be conceived separately. I thank you for the amount of work which you must have put into the writing of the criticism. I am sincerely sorry that the death of your father broke in upon your great work. Please accept my most sincere sympathies. I myself laid my daughter in her coffin with the last page of my *Jenufa*. I expect to be invited during next week to the full orchestral rehearsals. The stage, and what must take place there, will be a hard nut to crack.

With kindest regards,

Leoš Janáček.

Brno, 3th March, 1920.

To *Otakar Šourek.* Janáček's reply to Šourek's criticism of his *Excursions of Mr. Brouček*, which appeared in the magazine *Hudební revue*, No. 13. — Otakar Šourek (1883–), outstanding Czech writer on music and the biographer of Dvořák.

150. DIFFICULTIES WITH SINGERS

The part of Würfl in *Mr. Brouček* has damaged the resonance in the middle register of my voice. In other words, the main part of my voice. This means that I shall be unable to sing for several days. I take this opportunity of announcing to you my decision not to sing the part which I herewith return. I was engaged as a singer and not as a screamer, declamator, etc. I am also interested in keeping my voice as long as possible—who will give me anything if I lose it? No one, not a penny. Already, at the second rehearsal, I told the producer that I am unable to sing the part as it makes me hoarse, the cause being that the composer has no idea of the human voice and gives his singers impossible entries (bellowing and barking) which makes the voice suffer. I am not prepared to throw away all I have learned with such difficulty during fifteen years, for the sake of someone who has only to sit down and write notes easily with his pen, who is probably mad and does not care in the least whether his notes are singable or not.

From a letter written to the management of the National Theatre in Prague by *Václav Novák* (died 1928), baritone, quoted by *František Pala* in the magazine *Hudební Rozhledy*, Vol. VI, No. 18—19, 1953.

151. GRATITUDE TO A GOOD SINGER

Dear Sir,

I had seen the part of Mr. Brouček maliciously ruined, and now, in Brno I have seen the part played with lively natural gaiety. You played yourself entirely into the part without a single undue gesture: you managed to correspond completely with my idea of Mr. Brouček.

I am glad that he now runs about the stage in your person. There is now no need for me to worry about him any more. That is how it should be.
Thank you.

Yours sincerely,

Leoš Janáček.

Brno, 18th May, 1926.

A letter to *Valentin Šindler* (1885), tenor at the Brno Opera House from 1917 to 1932, where he sang the part of Mr. Brouček.

17. Janáček with the conductor, Sir Henry Wood, in London (1926).

18. Janáček with the wood-wind sextet in London (1926).

152. THE FIRST PERFORMANCE OF *THE EXCURSIONS OF MR. BROUČEK* IN PRAGUE

Janáček invited me to Prague for the first performance of the *Excursions of Mr. Brouček to the Moon and into the XVth Century*. The day of the first performance, the 23rd April, 1920, was my first visit to Prague. At 2 p. m. we met at the Hotel Imperial. Janáček was depressed in anticipation of the evening's performance, and was silent and absent-minded. I do not want to speak of the issue of the first performance, but of what happened during and after it. After the *Excursion to the Moon*, Janáček received, naturally in the wings, a beautiful bouquet of fresh roses. He thought that it had been given to him by the company and paid for out of the fund of the National Theatre in Brno. Considering this an unnecessary extravagance, he threw the bouquet wildly on the floor and muttered furiously to himself. Next day he heard from his wife that the bouquet had been sent to him by his niece. He went at once to visit her and begged her pardon.

Before the performance, we went together to choose a laurel wreath with long ribbon streamers for Ostrčil who was beginning his activities as conductor of the National Theatre in Prague with *The Excursions of Mr. Brouček*. After the performance the situation was most painful. No one took the slightest notice of Janáček. The official artistic world of Prague and the critics showed no interest in knowing anything about Janáček, although they had already heard his *Jenufa*. Therefore, there was no first-night celebration.

From the memoires of Janáček's pupil, *Osvald Chlubna* (1893—), which appeared in the theatre magazine, *Divadelní Listy* Brno, Vol. VII, 1931—1932. — *Janáček's niece*, mentioned in the above extract was Věra, daughter of Janáček's brother, Augustin.

153. FOR PROGRESS IN DRAMATIC ART

Dear friend,
Accept from me this wreath. You have lavished so much love and care on my work, that I can never repay you.

You have done a great service, I believe, to the progress of dramatic art. Not everyone is able to understand this.

Yours sincerely,

Leoš Janáček.

Prague, 23rd April, 1920.

From a letter to *Otakar Ostrčil*, written after the first performance of the *Excursions*.

154. A DANGEROUS SATIRE

While in Janáček's *Jenufa* the special melodic curves of speech which he uses are those of love, anguish, and tender reconciliation, in the *Excursion to the Moon* the curves most insisted upon are those of irony and sarcasm. It would be impossible to follow in detail all the intricate musical psychology of this part of *Mr. Brouček's Excursions*. There is a wide range of humour, from biting satire to broad farce.

The second part of Mr. Brouček's adventures, *The Excursions to the XVth Century*, although it is linked psychologically, and here and there musically, with the *Excursion to the Moon*, is very different in feeling from the almost extravaganza nonsense of the first picture of this diptych. The light if mordant satire of the moon-land adventure, becomes altogether more weighty and logical, even from the first bars of the orchestral Prelude with its rather tempestuous, evocation of a troubled past.

Musically this work is as valuable as either of Janáček's other operas. There are delightful musical moments in the first half and really great and salient pages in the second part. It has, however one serious fault which, in spite of its great musical merits, may for some time to come alienate the sympathy of its own people. As a satire *Mr. Brouček's Excursion to the XVth Century* has lost its point.

From an essay by *Rosa Newmarch* entitled *Leoš Janáček and Moravian Music-Drama* which appeared in the *Slavonic Review*, 1923.

155. LACK OF DRAMATIC UNITY

The opera, the *Excursions of Mr. Brouček*, was conceived as a satire which derided, in the person of Mr. Brouček, the petit bourgeois psychology with its vulgar and comic qualities; gluttony, drunkenness, boastfulness and cowardice. Under the influence of "one too many" (in the prologue) Mr. Brouček finds himself, during the first act, on the moon and, in the second act, under similar circumstances, in a cellar of Old Prague into which he has crashed and where he wakes up in the XVth Century during the Hussite wars. The life on the moon failed to satisfy Mr. Brouček because he could not get a proper drink there, nor a proper meal, and love was exclusively platonic. Still less can he accommodate himself to the war-time conditions of Hussite Prague, because war demands bravery and manly qualities—things quite foreign to his character. Finally, thrown out of the moon for drunkenness and incontinency in sexual matters, and with even greater disgrace, expelled from the turbulent Prague of the XVth century, for cowardice and unsuccessful vanity and boasting, Mr. Brouček is back in his own land. Not even here is he successful. He is thrust into a barrel and rolled off the scene. Such is this rather strange opera libretto, which carries visible traces of the modernistic trend of the early twenties.

The music leaves no doubt that it belongs to the modernistic European school of its time. It is exceedingly fragmentary, and one has a feeling that it might, at any moment, fall to pieces. The more or less clearly outlined melodic passages are drowned in a sea of declamatory semi-song, semi-dialogue. The orchestra is used mainly for purposes of illustration. The eclectic combinations of crude. Hussite chorals (second act) and light hearted "moon-waltzes" à la Richard Strauss' (first act) make one dissatisfied with the music. An abundance of orchestral effects, very clever in themselves, only emphasize the lack of that which makes a musical entity out of a composition.

From an article by *Dmitrij Kabalevsky* (1914–) which appeared in the magazine, *Music of the Soviet Union*, Vol. I, 1950.

156. HUSSITE HYMNS AND THE REVOLUTION.

During World War I, when the persecution of hungry workers caused a wave of strikes, Hussite ideas emerged again and again. It was the Moravian composer, Leoš Janáček, who of all the artists most pungently expressed the nation's desire for liberty. He did so in his opera, *The Excursion of Mr. Brouček to the XVth Century* (1917), and gave his personal opinion of that century in a letter to Mrs. Kamila Stössel written on the 17th October, 1917, one year before the end of World War I: "I am now steeped in exciting work. I am setting a story from the XVth century—the most sacred period for every Czech".

From these few characteristic words, Janáček's enthusiastic attitude to the Hussite movement is shown. Janáček was, from childhood, nationalistic and expressed this attitude often in terms which sometimes approached fanaticism. He was a "Hussite" of the Smetana type. Janáček wrote an article which appeared in the paper *Lidové Noviny* on the 23rd December, 1917 on his opera the *Excursion of Mr. Brouček to the XVth Century*, at a time when it was impossible to declare publicly his Hussite leanings. Yet even here his intention and ideas are clearly stated. He says: "A great day is approaching: will the shadows of doubt, weakness, unbelief and subjection be smoothed away from our brows? Will the star of hope shine forth? These thoughts were the firing impulse to work; the worse the time, the quicker the avalanche of ideas for composition. It is time for my work to be brought to life, it is time for it to speak!"

Janáček was completely immersed in the second half of his *Excursions of Mr. Brouček* because *The Excursion to the XVth Century* caused him far less difficulty with the librettists than he had experienced with the first half *(To the Moon)* and also because he longed to set an example, by the glorification of the Hussite movement, to all our weaklings and Oblomovs. As early as the 24th March, 1917, he writes to his librettist, František S. Procházka, who was always very willing to comply with his demands: "What if I asked you to dramatize the *Excursion into the XVth Century?* There is much truth in it. Heaps, in fact. And the whips can still be used on us with good effect. A new era will come; it is on its way. We must set up a well cleaned mirror on Vítkov hill, our pettiness is personified in Mr. Brouček—all ready-made for the stage." Janáček perhaps never worked with so much hope and pleasure as on this opera. He considered it to be a matter of importance to the Czechs and was convinced that it would never be translated. Later, he took a great deal of trouble to ensure that the figure of Jan Žižka of Trocnov was given its proper prominence. From the musical point of view the *Excursion of Mr. Brouček to the XVth Century* is important on account of its personal expression of the Hussite idea, and is certainly among the best works produced on this subject. If Smetana presents the Hussite movement in the prophecy of Libuše, and glorifies the Czech nation in the final chorus of that opera where he used the theme of "Ye Who Are God's Valiant Soldiers", Janáček expresses the Hussite movement in scenes where the main parts are given to the armed masses and in which their most revolutionary actions take place. This collective and fighting spirit, although typical, is a new way of considering the Hussite movement. The people are the executors of power and their will is expressed by the librettist in the following words: "Naught else can be done than to defend this truth to the last drop of blood, against the church, against the king, against the whole world..."

From my essay *Hussite Motives in Czech Music, and Music in General*. Published in the magazine of the Prague National Museum, 1953. — The widespread Hussite revolutionary movement was caused by the burning at the stake of John Hus, 6th July 1415, and struck the first blows at the feudal system in the Czech lands. This period, when the Hussite warriors, led by Jan Žižka of Trocnov, proceeded from the victory at Vítkov hill near Prague to further victories, has left deep traces both in music and in other works of art in Bohemia and abroad. —

157. CZECHOSLOVAKIA—THE HEART OF EUROPE

I come with the youthful spirit of my country, with youthful music. I am not one who likes to look back; on the contrary, I prefer to look ahead. I know that we have to grow, yet there is no growth in pain or in memories of oppression and suffering. Let us throw these off. Let us realise that we now have to look into the future. We are now a nation which should have a definite meaning in the world. "We are the heart of Europe." And Europe needs to be aware of its heart.

From a speech made by Janáček during his visit to England in 1926. Published in the magazine, *Listy Hudební Matice*, Prague, Vol. V, 1926, p. 257.

158. JANÁČEK'S PLANS

Dear Friend,

I should like to make an end of my life's work. *1.* As the Chairman of the Comission for the study of Czech folk songs in Moravia and Silesia (a Ministerial affaire), I have under my protection 10,000 folk songs. The first volume is ready for the press. *2.* The musical institution where I used to express my ideas on that subject, the School of Organists, was to have become an institute owned by the Moravian land-council. For 36 years I have been carrying the burden of this institution on my shoulders, and now 3. I would like to shift all these worries from my mind in order to be able to proceed, undisturbed, with my composing, in such a way as was suggested to me by you in your criticism written for the magazine, *Čas*, of *Maryčka Magdonová*. I will have to have a talk with the Minister of Culture and Education about these matters. I want to go next week, for this purpose, to Prague. Who could give me an introduction? Do you know him? Could you do it? This type of prelude achieves far more than could my brief interview. The request for the nationalisation and promotion of the above-mentioned institute to University status, to a Conservatoire, has been officially made in Brno in accordance with the opinions of all the most prominent members of Brno musical life. Enclosed you will find a lengthy petition addressed to Parliament.

With kindest regards,

Yours very sincerely,

Leoš Janáček.

Brno, 16th November, 1918.

To *Jan Herben*. — Soon after the end of World War I, Janáček began work on the founding of the Brno conservatoire. The School of Organists, of which he was director for almost 40 years, from 1881, was merged into the Conservatoire. — The letter to Jan Herben was published in *Lidové Noviny* on the 12th August 1938 by *Gracian Černušák* (1882–), music critic and historian.

159. AGAINST INSUFFICIENT EQUIPMENT OF A MUSICAL INSTITUTION

To the Ministry of Culture and Education.

Thanks to the memorandum issued by the State Conservatoire in Prague (No. 1842/22) I am able to state how the master-class in composition, Brno branch, is fitted out.

It is certain that without material such as:

1. all works recognised as being of the highest quality, as far as possible, in full score—
2. all scholarly literature concerning music—
3. all collections of folk songs—

4. technical equipment for scholarly analyses of composition—
5. a piano—
6. appropriate rooms with an atmosphere likely to stimulate invention.

Without these, the master-class in composition cannot exist.

The matter of a music college cannot be settled merely by the nomination of a professor.

Of all the equipment stated above, the master-class in composition, Brno branch, possesses nothing.

As early as 1919 on the 29th November, the Governing Board of the State Conservatoire in Brno decided that the master-class in composition should be equipped with Hipp's Chronoscope. The sum of 5000 crowns was allotted from the budget, to pay for this instrument. In the memorandum No. 55094, 5993, dated 10th December, the Ministry of Culture and Education recommended the cutting out of this expense. The Governing Body, in a memorandum of the 15th December, 1919, again asked for 5000 crowns for the purchase of Hipp's Chronoscope. The Ministry of Culture and Education made no reply. In 1921 I demanded, during a conference of professors of the master-classes in Prague, that the colleges should be allotted a definite sum for the purchase of teaching equipment. In 1922, I repeated this demand.

In 1922 the Ministry of Culture and Education rejected a request for a sum to be devoted to the purpose of purchasing teaching equipment. I therefore presented a list of the most necessary works for didactic purposes needed during the year 1922-1923. Up to this day, I have received nothing.

Finally, I must either borrow all the necessary equipment or buy it with my own money.

This leads me to the conclusion that ordinary students of the Conservatoire, who pay 148 crowns a term, are better catered for than students attending the master-class in composition who pay 800.

Leoš Janáček.

Brno, 18th November, 1922.

A copy of this memorandum addressed to the Ministry of Culture and Education was sent to me by the composer *Josef Bohuslav Foerster* (1859–1951), who received it from Janáček. This memorandum is a good example of how Janáček conceived the equipment necessary for the master-class of the State Conservatoire and how he fought for its high standard. Janáček was professor of the master-class of the Prague Conservatoire, Brno branch, from the 25th November, 1919 until the 11th February, 1925 when he retired.

160. GRATITUDE TO FERDINAND VACH

Dear Friend,

I am writing to you immediately after the concert. Thank you for your trouble. You have done a great deal of honest work. You are a man of action and of few words. That is as it should be. I am sure that we are going to meet more and more often. We are following the same road. When "Belvedere" gets into the skins of the performers, it will make, when added to "Golden Street", three items which will, I hope, be a success. Give my regards to the whole choir and stand your ground in this flood of "young" sounds. Once more, my sincerest thanks.

Yours ever,

Leoš Janáček.

Brno, 25th November, 1918.

A letter to *Ferdinand Vach.* — Janáček wrote this letter immediately after a concert given by the Moravian Women-Teachers' Choir in Brno on the 25th November 1918 when Vach conducted the *Songs from Hradčany—Belvedere, Golden Street* and *The Weeping Fountain*, which were composed in 1916.

161. JANÁČEK AND THE BRNO OPERA HOUSE

When, after World War I, the City Theatre passed into the hands of the National Theatre Society, I did my utmost to ensure that the new era should be introduced by one of Janáček's operas.

Janáček's artistic personality became the banner and the password of our new temple of dramatic art. Five years have now passed and I am pleased to be able to state that this banner has led us the right way and that it will continue to lead us still further towards our highest aims.

These aims are for me, first and foremost, in Janáček's original ideas. Our theatre must differentiate itself from the others as much through its repertoire as through its performances. Janáček never bothered about how other composers worked. Neither did we ape other leading theatres, but went our own way, which was often far from easy. Our example was Janáček's progressiveness, honesty, capacity for work, his sincerity in art and the ruggedness of his forms; and his maxims; less words—more music, modest means—great effects, and the common speech—the nation's art.

From an article by *František Neumann* (1874–1929) entitled *Leoš Janáček and Our Theatre*, which was published in the magazine *Divadelní Šepty Národního divadla v Brně*, Vol. V., 1924–1925. — *František Neumann* became director of the opera in the Brno National Theatre in the Spring of 1919. He began his activities by producing Janáček's *Jenufa*.

162. JANÁČEK AND NEUMANN

Janáček once said: "I have seen my works on the stages of the world, but I must say that this Neumann, after all, produces them best". In this utterance is perhaps the highest praise that Janáček ever gave. It is a fact that Janáček greatly loved and esteemed all who attached themselves to his works. Nevertheless, occasionally a dissonance was struck in the harmony between Janáček and Neumann. Yet it was never more than temporary. For instance, shortly before the first night of *Káťa Kabanová*, Neumann threw the score on the floor. Janáček calmly and without a word picked it up, took it home, and sat up, late into the night, correcting the mistakes which the irresponsible copyist had made. Janáček never mentioned this event, except once when he told me, with a sigh: "In the beginning I couldn't be expected to see how many mistakes there were, but just listen; and how plainly they could be heard!" That was all. Today, in all fairness we may say that Janáček made Neumann, but also that Neumann made Janáček, and that the Brno theatre was the gate through which Janáček's works went out into the world, the begining of his world-wide renown.

From an article by *Osvald Chlubna* which appeared in the magazine, *Divadelní list*, Brno, Vol. VII, 1931–1932.

163. THE DIARY OF ONE WHO VANISHED

The Diary of One who Vanished, is an expression of Janáček's attachment to social and folk motives. In the *Diary* he demonstrated the necessity of giving every human being his due, even gipsies, wrongly considered to be a race of out-casts. Taken with an article in the paper "Lidové Noviny" published in Brno and entitled "From the Pen of a Self-Taught Poet", his sympathies were roused by the story of the village youth who fell in love with a dark gipsy girl and went off with her. The moral and human character of the young man, who was ready to make every sacrifice for his love, made a great impression on Janáček. He was himself under the strong influence of a true and deep affection for Mrs. Kamila Stössel (1892—1935), whom he had met at Hukvaldy in 1915 and with whom he had later formed a close friendship at the Spa of Luhačovice (from 1917 onwards). Under these circumstances, he was able to master with far greater reality the glowingly lyrical and yet highly dramatic words.

From his letters to Mrs. Stössel we can follow Janáček's work on the *Diary*. As early as the 10th August, 1917, he writes to her: "Regularly, every afternoon, something makes me think of a few motives for those beautiful verses about the gipsy love. Perhaps it will make a nice musical novel, and perhaps there will be a scrap of the Luhačovice atmosphere in it."

Janáček, till the end of his life, became more and more attached to Mrs. Stössel, and as his attachment grew, he projected more and more of his feelings into his works. In the *Diary*, he underlined and portrayed her sympathetic attitude to people in general. In one of his letters and also in a newspaper article he writes: "You were the one I thought of when writing this work. You were the gipsy, Zefka. Zefka, with the child in her arms and he following her. They all know you in Písek in the quarter down by the mill-bank, where you clothed and fed the gipsy children. The little ones fell into the trap of your heart."

These were the main social and sentimental motives which contributed to the creation of a work so exuberant with feeling as is *The Diary of One who Vanished*. The same is demonstrated by the composer's attitude to the text which entirely bewitched him.

From the vocal point of view the whole work is a beautiful example of the monothematic development of a melodic idea, growing mainly from a perfect fourth and a major second which run alternately up and down. This melodic idea had already appeared in Janáček's earlier works, especially in the *Excursions of Mr. Brouček*. In the *Diary*, however, it reaches its highest concentration.

The most important thing for Janáček in his work was to lay stress on the dramatic tension and verve. The *Diary* is, in reality, a miniature drama that could be very well staged. Janáček demands for its performance dim lighting, an unobtrusive entrance and exit of the contralto, and no breaks, not even pauses between the individual sections. All twenty-two sections form a perfectly joined, dramatic and balanced whole, dominated by the glow of the extremely difficult tenor part, the sensually attractive colour of the contralto voice and the enchanting mood evoked by the narrative women's chorus. The piano part completes the musical drama which, by its form, eruptive quality and difficulty, is unique in "Lieder" literature at home and abroad.

From my foreword to the second edition of Janáček's *The Diary of One who Vanished*, Prague, 1953.

164. ADMIRER OF RUSSIAN LITERATURE

Janáček's sixth opera, *Káťa Kabanová*, written in the years 1919-1921 was his first to be composed after the forming of the Czechoslovak State. In it, Janáček once more expressed his love for the strengh of the Russian people.

His affectionate attitude to Russia is today generally known, as is that of other members of his family. His brothers, František and Josef, the school-master, lived there for many years. The children of Josef Janáček settled in Russia for good. Janáček's nephew, Vladimír, lived in Volynia (Zdolbunovo); another nephew, Leo, lived in the Ukraine in the Kharkov district (Kramatorsk); and his niece, Olga, was settled in Moscow. Janáček almost became Director of the Warsaw Conservatoire (1904). He was so strongly pro-Russian and so attracted by Russian revolutionary and romantic literature that he alternated Russian and Czech themes as subjects for his compositions.

In the 'twenties he began composing with great intensity. His main attention was concentrated on giving the nation operas which were new in style and expression and on being, before all, an operatic composer. He was certainly aware of the fact that Brno was going through struggles similar to those which Smetana had lived through in Prague, when his generation fought for the realism and the progressiveness of a new operatic style. Janáček therefore put forward all his strength, especially as he was approaching his 70th birthday. Yet his genius and art grew, and he guarded the individuality of his creations at all costs. Between the years 1919-1928, that is, during the last nine years of his life, he produced four operas and re-wrote a fifth, besides writing his great Glagolic Mass, two string quartets a wind sextet, *Youth*, a set of *Nursery Rhymes*, a Concertino for Piano and Chamber Orchestra, a Capriccio for Piano with the left hand and small orchestra, and the *Symphonietta* for full orchestra, many revisions of former compositions, and engaded in literary activities and tours. Janáček's time had come and the time was ripe for Janáček.

From my article which appeared in the theatre magazine, *Divadelní list*, Opava, No. IX, 1953.

165. THE OPERA *KÁŤA KABANOVÁ*

After unusually hard work, I have finished my latest opera. I do not know yet whether I shall call it *The Storm* or *Katěrina*. The fact that there already exists an opera called *The Storm*, influences me against using that title, and against calling it *Katěrina* is the fact that I keep writing nothing but women! *Jenufa-Katěrina*. The best thing would be to use three asterisks instead of a title.

Brno, 6th March, 1921.

From a letter to *Mrs. Kamila Stössel*.

166. AGAINST THE DECADENT SOCIETY OF OLD RUSSIA

Janáček's trip to Russia in 1896 probably gave rise to this oppressive drama written to the words of the famous play by Ostrovský, *The Storm*. In this work the life of Old Russia is portrayed against the background of a small country-town, Kalinov, a hundred years ago. The merciless tradition, the family despotism, the slavery of a married woman, the bigoted religious attitude, the senseless superstitions, the many severe regulations which held people bound as though in an iron corselet—all this is embodied in the person of the old mother Kabanikha who, in the name of tradition, tyrannizes her son, her daughter-in-law, her friends and the whole of her surroundings. This is the source of a sequence of dramatic scenes. Against all this the libretto presents, in sharp constrast, a couple of unprejudiced lovers—the student Kudryash and Varvara, his girl, whom he has inculcated with in his ideas. Throughout the work, these two young people heap their sarcasm on the old-fashioned way of life, and those representing it. Finally, disgusted with this type of society, they abandon the town and set out to seek their happiness in the big city. The desire for freedom breaks all fetters. Janáček wrote beautiful music to this libretto, music expressing with harmonies of terror and despotism all that was Old Russia and, with the most beautiful melodies, the love of the emancipated lovers. The main theme of the work appearing in the beginning of the overture is most important. The Czech and German critics imagined it to be the theme of Tikhon's departure. In reality, however, it represents Old Russia, the iron bands of tradition, and appears about fifty times unchanged during the work. It is presented in many varied tempos, yet always with the same domineering rhythm, mostly on ff timpani. This theme also closes the work, forming the last bar. On hearing these eight notes, our blood runs cold. The second important theme in the opera *Káťa Kabanová*, the theme of Varvara, changes sometimes into a folk tune, for instance, in the beautiful garden nocturne. This theme appears for the last time when Varvara decides to flee with her lover from the small town. We may say that Janáček, although he was sixty-seven years old, worked on this theme *Con amore*, a fact which may be considered as proving that the couple Kudryash and Varvara had won his entire sympathy. The opera is an oppressive drama whose music, in spite of the shortcomings of the libretto, is so beautiful that it will certainly rank next to *Jenufa* in Janáček's work.

From a book about Janáček by the French writer, *Daniel Muller*, Paris 1930, Editions Rieder.

167. JANÁČEK'S "CON AMORE"

Dear Kamila,

It was in the sunshine of summer. The sun-warmed slope of the hill where the flowers wilted.

That was when the first thoughts about poor *Káťa Kabanová* and her great love came to my mind. She calls to the flowers, she calls to the birds—flowers to bow down to her, birds to sing for her the last song of love.

"Dear friend" I said to Professor Knop, "I know a most wonderful lady. I have her perpetually in my mind. My Káťa grows in her, in Kamila! This will be the most gentle and tender of my works."

And so it came to pass. I never met greater love than in her. Through her may it be blessed. Flowers, bow down to her! Birds, cease not your songs of eternal love!

Leoš Janáček, Ph.D.

Písek, 12th February, 1928.

Janáček's inscription on the title page of the piano score of *Káťa Kabanová* which was preserved in the town of Písek. A proof of his affection for Mrs. Kamila Stössel which developed in Písek. — Janáček wrote *Káťa Kabanová* during the years 1919–1921 based on an adaptation of *The Storm* by *A. N. Ostrovsky* (1823–1886). — Instead of *Knop*, Janáček meant *Khodl*, whom he used to meet in Písek.

168. THE STRUGGLE FOR ARTISTIC PROGRESS IN BRNO

Dear Friend,

We have met several times without any previous arrangement during an artistic performance, just as water and lightning meet. The production of *Káťa Kabanová* is one of such meetings. It seems that Brno is back in Smetana's days. Am I to thank you or the or-

19. The National Theatre at Bratislava, where *Káťa Kabanová*, conducted by Milan Zuna, was successfully performed in 1923.

20. The Moravian Teachers' Chorus with their conductor Prof. Vach made Janáček famous abroad even before his *Jenufa* was performed.

chestra or the singers? We are all happy that each one of us has developed in his own way. We are able to honour and love each other mutually.

To all who contributed to the performance of *Kátá Kabanová*, I am

Your sincerely devoted

Leoš Janáček.

Brno, 27th November, 1921.

Janáček's letter to *František Neumann*, the director of the National Theatre in Brno, written after the first performance of *Kátá Kabanová* on the 23rd November, 1921. — Compare my article, *Janáček and Neumann*, which appeared in the magazine, *Smetana*, No. I, Vol. XXXIV, Prague, 12th April, 1942, p. 73.

169. GRATITUDE TO THE SLOVAK NATIONAL THEATRE IN BRATISLAVA

I attended the first performance of *Kátá Kabanová* in Bratislava. It was the best production of this work of mine which I have yet seen. Better than in Brno and better than in Prague. I took a fancy to Bratislava. Brno hates me. Prague envies me, but in Bratislava they welcome me. A very nice old town, the swift Danube...

From a letter to *Mrs. Kamila Stössel*, written on the 3rd April, 1923.

170. *KÁTÁ KABANOVÁ* IN OSTRAVA

Dear Sir,

We intend in the near future to begin rehearsing your opera *Kátá Kabanová*. We request your kind permission to perform it and your consent to our obtaining the necessary material. We would like to assure you, dear Sir, that the director of our opera, Mr. Emanuel Bastl, will give the performance all his attention so that it may bring due honour to the work. We hope that you will not refuse your permission and shall be glad if you could let us know, through the producer, Mr. Kühn, of any special wishes which you might have. Hoping to hear from you at your earliest convenience,

> Yours very sincerely,
> The Management of the National Theatre
> in Moravská Ostrava.

October 25th, 1923.

A letter to Leoš Janáček. The manager of the above theatre was, at that time, František Uhlíř. — *Emanuel Bastl* (1874–1950) was from 1916 conductor and from 1919 to 1926 director of the opera house in Moravská Ostrava. — *Jan Kühn* (1892–) was stage director at the same opera house.

To the Management of the National Theatre in Moravská Ostrava.

It will be a pleasure to see you produce my *Káťa Kabanová*! If you go through the repertoire of our theatres—then it is obvious that living composers have only one hope, at least after their deaths, etc. etc.

> Yours very sincerely,
> *Leoš Janáček.*

Brno, 27th October, 1923.

Janáček's answer to the management of the National Theatre in Moravská Ostrava

171. IMPORTANCE OF A GOOD PRODUCTION

We certainly attended an important event in our cultural life in last night's first performance of *Káťa Kabanová*, where the composer, a native of this district, Mr. Janáček, was present. We were curious to know how satisfied he was with the performance and we asked him for his opinion in a short interview. I think that we all, especially the members of the National Theatre of Moravian Silesia, can be satisfied with his verdict. After the successes of *Káťa Kabanová* in Brno, Prague, Bratislava and Cologne, the work has now been performed in Moravská Ostrava. Mr. Janáček first of all praised the excellent production of Mr. Kühn. According to Janáček the perfect balance of the ensemble, where every dramatic moment found its reflection in the expressions of the entire cast, is due mainly to the great work of the producer. This achieved a climax in the last act and Mr. Janáček declared that the final scene had never been so well produced as in our theatre. With the same praise he mentioned the interpreter of Káťa Kabanová, Mrs. Šmíd. According to him she acted "extremely well and it was obvious that she was singing with all her soul". We were pleased to hear him give our orchestra its due after the excellent playing under the baton of Mr. Bastl. Janáček told us that he had been afraid that our orchestra might be too weak. Yet with our limited resources, the orchestra played well and with such finish "that there was not a single wrong note". The theatre was packed out and this made the orchestra sound even better. "The music seemed to come from my own heart. I am happy. It gripped me."

From an article which appeared in the paper *Moravsko–Slezský deník* on the 19th January 1924.

172. HOW *FOX SHARPEARS* CAME INTO BEING

Fox Sharpears has played her tricks even in the newspapers. I do not know why people like her so much. Perhaps because she keeps well to the ground.

It would never have occurred to me to imagine that she had a diligent reader and an admirer, a man with silver hair and sparkling eyes. I know him only distantly because he is a musician and I do not pretend to understand music. Suddenly I heard that the fox had bewitched him and that he wanted her trivial words and even more trivial actions transcribed into the language of notes which is, of all human things, the least earth-bound.

I could not believe it and took it for a joke. Later I was attacked by a direct demand: what would I have to say to it. I said nothing. I was surprised and had the feeling that someone wanted to play a trick even on me. Then, one spring day two years ago, I received an invitation from Janáček himself.

My heart was heavier than the heart of Sharpears when she was caught in the larder during a village feast. I gathered together all my courage and went. It was a May day, and the song of the birds filled the air over the streets and roofs of Brno as if it had been somewhere in the meadows down by the Svitava river.

Leoš Janáček was waiting for me in the small garden of the Conservatoire. He sat among the bushes, with thousands of tiny blossoms shining round his head; that head of his was equally white, and seemed to be the biggest of those flowers. He smiled; and I immediately knew that this is the smile which life presents to us like a gold medal for bravery in the face of the enemy; for bravery in sorrow, adversity and hatred. At that moment I believed that Fox Sharpears was sitting, tamed and quite dominated by the kindness of the man in the small garden, and that she would approach unseen to sit at our feet and listen to our plotting. Janáček mentioned the story in a few words and then began talking about the forest at his home in Wallachia which I do not know. He talked about his studies of birds chirping and I realised that he knew the happiness contained in his smile.

From the memoires of *Rudolf Těsnohlídek* (1882–1928), published under the title *The Youthful Sage*, in *Lidové Noviny*, July 3rd, 1924. Janáček's seventh opera *The Adventures of Fox Sharpears*, 1923, is based on a story by Rudolf Těsnohlídek.

Dear Friend,

I remember what happened in my native village.

The village Mayor's son, in a fit of passion—his girl had deserted him—almost slaughtered all the wedding guests. He shot at them through the windows of the room where the marriage of his former sweetheart was taking place.

He was accused and sentenced.

That would not be surprising. But when, after having served his sentence, he returned to the village, do you suppose the people avoided him?

No. Just as though nothing had happened.

They treated him in exactly the same way as before.

This, to me, was a proof that the simple people do not consider evil as a lasting stain. For them it was, and is no more.

The same may be said for my Fox Sharpears: she pilfered and killed, yet in spite of it all she is capable of generous feelings.

In the second act she leads the life of a tramp. She chases the badger out of his den and settles in his warm layer. She spends her nights in pubs, she steals and plays various tricks on the school master and the parson who are returning, tipsy, from the village inn.

The fox falls deeply in love.

The schoolmaster declares his love to the blossom of a sunflower leaning over a fence, the parson recalls his student affections. Everywhere there is Fox Sharpears.

The forester, the last one to leave the inn, scares her away with a wild shout and a gun-shot.

The schoolmaster and the parson scramble to their feet and try as hard as they can to get off the stage.

In the third act, Fox Sharpears has a great many of her cubs around her. Family bliss.

A poultry vendor who is also a poacher rests with his basket of poultry in the forest. Fox Sharpears has a little game with him.

She shows herself, and the poacher is after her with a gun. They chase each other. The cubs, meanwhile make short work of the poultry. "What, you want to kill me, just because I'm a fox," she shouts at the poacher. His hair stands on end when he sees his basket red with little foxes. He shoots without aiming and that is the end of Fox Sharpears.

The forester and the schoolmaster have grown old. The parson has moved to some other place.

Spring is in the woods—yet old age is also apparent.

The forest with all its animal folk appears in a dream to the forester. The old man seeks his Sharpears but she is gone. Then suddenly a little cub, exactly like Sharpears comes gambling to his feet. "Just like her mother."

And so evil and good make their round through life anew.

From Janáček's letter to *Max Brod* written on the 11th March, 1923. From the *Correspondence of Leoš Janáček and Max Brod*, Prague, 1953.

174. IN PRAISE OF NATURE AND ETERNAL LIFE

Apart from the revolutionary and folk motives there are, threaded through the opera, epic, satirical and lyrical moments. The lyric parts are at their best when Janáček wants to evoke Spring, the forest and the magic of night. Equally, the courting of Sharpears, the love scenes and the final epilogue of the forester (is it a fairy-tale or reality?) are among the most lyrical and melodious passages in Janáček's works. He almost always expresses himself at these moments with a love motive which is a mere fourth and major second running alternately up and down. Yet the May motive is the most dominating; when nature buds and blossoms. With this motive, Janáček bade farewell to Sharpears with a hymn to nature, to mother earth and to the eternal changing and regeneration of life, whose innermost foundation is love.

This is the essence of Janáček's greatness. The opera is gay with a sad ending (the fox receives a fatal wound), but nature has taken care of the new life and Janáček celebrates this new life with the melody of the May motive, with the melody of love and of Spring giving birth to perpetually regenerated life.

From my article on Janáček's *Fox Sharpears* which appeared in the magazine of the County Theatre in Plzeň, 1953.

175. NERVOUS STRAIN DURING REHEARSALS

One might almost say that the National Theatre in Brno could not keep pace with Janáček's output of opera. There was always a new one waiting for its first night. Brno knows how to perform Janáček. It is his town. It loved him and honoured him a whole ten years sooner than the rest of the world. Janáček's contact with opera there was very intimate. He often attended rehearsals and he was present at almost every performance. What a presence! He paced up and down or stood speechless in the wings, steeped in thought as if in deep meditation. He never talked to anyone and no one addressed him. It seemed as if his attitude towards the theatre as a living body was almost indifferent. Yet this was far from the case. Everyone knew it, everyone made a silent bow and went on with his work. After all, time was scarce and Janáček knew it. His presence was a natural thing to everyone. He belonged to the theatre as much as the producer or the stage-hands or the electricians or a part of the set. He was silent—here probably he experienced moments of real calmness and peace.

From an article by *Dr. Jiří Svoboda* (1897–), Brno composer, which was published in the magazine, *Hudba a škola*, Vol. I., 1928–1929.

176. THE PRAGUE PRODUCTION OF *FOX SHARPEARS*

They have produced my *Fox Sharpears* but not as I would have wished. I had been looking forward to it for months, yet it did not come off as I had expected. One thing is certain; you cannot persuade anyone with art. It is like beating an eiderdown with your fist, it merely bulges somewhere else. They applaud everything. And yet there is only one truth in music. A truth which everyone is after but which only a few have attained.

Brno, 21st May 1925.

From a letter to *Mrs. Kamila Stössel* written after a performance of *Fox Sharpears* at the National Theatre in Prague on the 18th May, 1925.

177. 70-YEAR OLD JANÁČEK'S PRAISE FOR PRAGUE

My dear Lord Mayor,

You congratulate me on behalf of the city of Prague and on your own behalf on my 70th birthday. Prague, which has attracted my heart since I was a boy and where I spent the bitter years of my studies and which I thank for the rise of my star. I am grateful, my Lord Mayor, that you in your high position remember me, a simple composer.

I thank you most sincerely.

Yours very respectfully,

Leoš Janáček.

Hukvaldy, 14th July 1924.

Janáček's letter to the Lord Mayor of Prague, *Dr Karel Baxa* (1863–1938), kept in the Archives of the city of Prague, No. 14/II, 25 pres. First published by me in the fortnightly magazine, *Národní Divadlo*, Vol. XVIII, No. 9, on the 26th February, 1941.

178. INSPIRED BY LIFE AND NATURE

Dear Friend,

We rarely meet in the streets of Brno. It is obvious that each one of us seeks a special corner for his thoughts. I thank you for remembering me. I cannot say of myself that I have won the game. Neither do I know whether I shall play to the end. There is not enough done for me to be fully contained in my work. You authors are able to tell everything with words, although I do not play about with empty melodies. I dip them in life and nature. I find work very difficult and serious—perhaps for this reason.

With kindest regards,

Yours sincerely,

Leoš Janáček.

Hukvaldy, 15th July, 1924.

Enclosed you will find a very nice *ex libris* by Milén.

From a letter to *Karel Elgart Sokol* (1874—1929), a Brno author. — *Eduard Milén* (b. 1891), Czech painter.

179. HIS 70TH ANNIVERSARY

I remember that one of the happiest days of his life was the day he celebrated his 70th birthday in 1924. That was the day I persuaded him to write his memoires and his valuable remarks about his musical work. At that period I used to be a daily guest at the Janáčeks' house. Both the sitting-room and the study were an equally interesting sight. The sitting-room looked like a glass house: wreaths, fresh and fading, bouquets and garlands of silver painted laurel of all sizes decorated with red and blue ribbons; diplomas, souvenirs and many other presents, all trophies of the anniversary concerts and anniversary opera performances. And the study? Here and there a few smaller additions to the trophies but the most noticeable object was the big black piano. There it stood as if in expectation, with the keyboard open and a score on which he was working, scrawled over with corrections, crossings out,

quick sketches and alterations, left prepared on the music stand...
typical work by Leoš Janáček and a hard nut to crack for the
copyist and for the unfortunate person who had to make the piano
score. It was his new opera, the *Makropulos Secret*, and beside it lay
the play by Karel Čapek which Janáček had changed, cut and re-
arranged as was his custom with every one of his texts.

The year of his anniversary was happily over. It culminated
with the writing of two works about Janáček; with the discovery
of the *Wallachian Dances* and *Šárka*; with his receiving an honorary
doctorate and with the full recognition of his art by the general
musical public. It was no light matter, this half year of constant
tension. Several times, Mrs. Janáček and I became seriously worried
about his health. It is a good thing to be mentally and physically
fit, but 70 years are, after all, 70 years.

From an article by *Adolf Veselý*, *My Last Conversation with Leoš Janáček*, published in
1924 in the magazine, *Hudební Rozhledy*, Vol. IV, 1928, No. 4—8. — *Adolf Veselý* wrote a book
no Janáček in collaboration with Max Brod. — *Wallachian* (corr. *Lachian*) *Dances* were composed in 1889—1890.

180. HIS BIOGRAPHY

Dear Friend,

Your book has quite rejuvenated me. Thank you with all my
heart for your work. I can see in the book how a human life can
be compressed into a few pages, as if the pages had wings; how far
will they yet fly!

Yours,

Leoš Janáček.

Brno, 27th January, 1925.

Janáček's letter of thanks to *Adolf Veselý* who published in Prague in 1924 the mono-
graph for Janáček's 70th birthday under the title, *Leoš Janáček, a Glimpse into His Life and Work.*

181. QUARTET INSPIRED BY TOLSTOI

I have never heard anything so wonderful as the way the "Bohemian Quartet" played my work. When the headmaster, who is a musician, comes to see you, remind him to invite the "Bohemian Quartet" to Písek so that the people there may hear it. I myself was thrilled and it is over a year since I wrote it.

I had in mind an unhappy, tortured, beaten woman, beaten to death as Tolstoi described her in his *Kreutzer Sonata*.

They play it on Friday and again on Monday—and they will play it all over the world!

My very best wishes. You are often in my thoughts.

Leoš Janáček.

Prague, 14th October 1924.

From a letter to his friend *Mrs Kamila Stössel* telling how his Quartet (1923) was inspired by Tolstoi's story, *Kreutzer Sonata*.

182. HONORARY DOCTOR OF THE MASARYK UNIVERSITY IN BRNO

Rector Magnificus,

On this memorable day for our University, I address you on behalf of the Professors of the Faculty of Arts, requesting you to be so kind as to accept the chairmanship at this significant celebration of our Alma Mater. Today will be the first time that, according to the old and honorable tradition, the Masaryk University bestows the degree of Honorary Doctor on a man who with his activities has achieved splendid results in furthering the culture of the whole nation, and thus, outside the sphere of the University, has gained what the Alma Mater honours and pursues as her highest aim. We are happy to be able to bestow this honour on a personality who throughout the long years has combined artistic enthusiasm with deep moral sincerity, high international standards and the fresh spirit of the homeland and, what is perhaps more precious, the creative endeavour of a musician breaking new ground in art with the scientific mind of a collector, theoretician and scholar fulfilling the aims of a long tradition. With him there enters into Czech musical art a new Moravian, Eastern element.

From a speech by the Dean of the Faculty of Arts of the Masaryk University, *Arne Novák* (1870—1939), delivered when Janáček received his honorary degree.

183. CONGRATULATIONS FROM JOSEF SUK

Dear Doctor Janáček, Maestro,

I would like to congratulate you on behalf of the professorial staff of the Conservatoire, on behalf of the members of the Czech Composers' Club as well as on behalf of the "Hudební Matice" and the musical branch of the "Umělecká Beseda".

You have lived to see yourself rewarded with the highest honour that can be bestowed on a living artist, and to see yourself respected by the present day musical world which feels itself honoured by your presence.

I very often recall — and especially on this occasion — the memorable first performance — or almost the first performance — of your *Jenufa* in Prague. We all felt that it was a success not only of a work of local importance but of a work that will become our pride in the eyes of the world.

After the first act we said to ourselves "here we have an author who loves mankind and feels compassion for it."

Your creative power has shone brightly forth since that time and you have given us works of equal importance, yet each time new and dear to us: all of them works of love and compassion whether they be an outcry or contain a smile of kindness.

Maryčka Magdonová, The 70.000, The Everlasting Gospel, The Fiddler's Child, The Diary of One who Vanished, Kát'a Kabanová, The Wandering Madman, Taras Bulba — what an amount of love and compassion is crammed into these powerful works. I shall never forget the way you confessed to the "Bohemian Quartet", during a rehearsal, that your inspiration for the work they were playing had been compassion for an unhappy, down-trodden woman.

You have reached the stage when you can sing of youth in blithe and glowing tones; and with a wise smile you glorify nature, the mother of people and animals whose hearts beat with one and the same rhythm. What a rich and instructive journey your life has made, and yet whenever I remember Jenufa's first night I cannot refrain from bitter thoughts. How long you had to live among us misunderstood.

There is someone in Jenufa who says that every couple must endure its sorrows. You have set this sentence to music most wonderfully. Not only each couple, but each man and woman and especially a creative artist must endure a certain amount of sorrow. You have done this and outlived it as you have outlived the days when you were unknown and misunderstood.

Today you must certainly be aware that we all gather round you with respect and love. This victory of your work is most gratifying and most instructive.

Although you have retired from your teaching activities, you continue to teach not only us but also the whole nation your many virtues:

You are teaching us to believe in our own strength.

You are teaching us to be patient when we do not achieve immediate success.

You are teaching us to long for constant progress, to fill our hearts with love and compassion, never to cease when one thing has been achieved but to seek, with pride and self-assurance, new paths and new truths.

173

May you remain in this our teacher for the future and may destiny grant you all the necessary health and strength.

From an address by *Josef Suk*, Rector of the Prague Conservatoire, delivered when Janáček received his degree of Doctor of Philosophy. — Compare *The Living Words of Josef Suk*, edited by *J. M. Kvĕt*.

184. JANÁČEK'S CREED

Dear Sirs,

As you have signed so unanimously the address of congratulation, let me thank you all at the same time. In the book of my life you are to read:

> Grow out of your innermost selves
> Never renounce your beliefs
> Do not toil for recognition
> But always do all you can
> So that the field alloted to you
> May prosper.

> Best wishes,
> Yours.
> *Leoš Janáček*, Ph. D.

Brno, 12th February, 1925.

Janáček's reply to an address from the members of the Ostrava musical societies given on the occasion of his receiving his honorary doctorate from the Brno University on the 28th January, 1925.

185. BEZRUČ'S CONGRATULATION

> Music is outside my ken;
> The virtuoso plays to a Barbarian.
> But the homely sounds of Ostravica
> And the cry of anguish of my country

Sped to me from every note of yours—
Hard indeed 'twould be to find its like!
Master, may you live for many years
To delight us and to move our tears!

From a letter written by *Petr Bezruč* to *Adolf Veselý*, dated Brno, 27th October, 1924, published in Veselý's book on Janáček. — In this letter Bezruč quotes the congratulation he sent to Janáček.

186. TWO GREAT ARTISTS

Dear Friend,

You are the one I have not yet thanked for remembering my anniversary.

Your lines pleased me very much; you are the only one among all the artists, writers, painters, sculptors, etc., etc., who have peeped into the lane where it thunders with music, and there you found me.

We are said to have once stood beside each other unknowigly. I feel myself near to you in spirit and yet we have never met.

Your verses came to hand just at the right moment. I wrapped them up in a resounding storm of anger, desperation and pain. Just the other day, I got news of how the Swedes, the Norwegians and the English are mad about our *70.000*.

Misery understands. And what is peculiar, the Germans in the Russian sector also sympathize.

Under our skies, from Babi Hura down to the Silesian lowlands, one may breathe again.

We have gone through a lot—there was always the one Idea in common. Thank you sincerely for remembering—and if Mr. Adolf Veselý prints your lines, let him print mine next to them.

They could not tear us apart.

With best wishes,

Yours,

Leoš Janáček.

Brno, 1st October, 1924.

A letter to the Czech poet, *Petr Bezruč*, reproduced in the book edited by *Adolf Veselý* on Janáček. — *70.000* is Janáček's male-voice choir composed to Bezruč's words. It was often sung by the Prague and Moravian Teachers' Choirs on their tours abroad.

187. SUCCESS ABROAD

Berlin, 15th March, 1924.

It has long been generally known that Bohemia reached a high-water mark in music with Smetana's *Bartered Bride*. Yet there now exists an opera which is more contemporary in spirit, or rather, more firmly rooted in the present day idiom. Leoš Janáček has gone a long way in building up the traditional theme with a free progressive spirit. It can be compared only with the first Russian operas, *Boris Godunov*, etc. It stands alone not only in the history of music, but especially in the history of opera. The success was tremendous.

Bremen, 15th November, 1925.

There is no question about his being a giant in his own field. Unusual declamation, true to nature, produces a lively dialogue, which comes directly from the soul. The whole is pervaded with intimate warmth, and the musical colour holds its own against the colours of the settings and costumes.

Magdeburg, 4th December, 1925.

The work of a truly creative imagination. Music which wells up from the heart. Clean, rich, warm, truthful and original music, which therefore lives and will continue to live.

Hamburg, 1st March, 1926.

A real work of art, humane in spirit, and of mythical power. The events develop with masterful logic and clarity. The dialogues

21. The Bohemian Quartet as caricatured by the painter Hugo Böttinger (1923), first interpreters of Janáček's string quartet written under the influence of the *Kreutzer Sonata* by Tolstoy.

22. Janáček (Photo from 1924).

are of high poetic force. The characters are endowed with an inner glow and are perfectly outlined. The final success develops as if of its own accord.

Posen, 10th April, 1926.

The success was brilliant. *Jenufa* was received in Posen with open arms and we can only be happy about it.

Lwow, 6th April, 1926.

The opera is filled to such an extent with original ideas and creative musical power, that Janáček presents himself as one of the most outstanding musicians of the present day.

Erfurt, 13th May, 1926.

One of the most powerfully dramatic works of this century. A veristic opera of immediate theatrical appeal. A musical drama of the highest concentration. A high-water mark in naturalistic opera, drawing its strength from the age-old springs of folk life. Written long before the eclectic and refined *Tiefland* and before the unhealthy, overwrought *Salome*, it is becoming the sensational success of the European stage.

From criticisms of the production of *Jenufa* in Germany and Poland.

188. KLEIBER CONDUCTS *JENUFA*

Dear Sir,

I am still with you in my thoughts. You felt the moments of climax in my work and presented them bright as with sunshine.

They used to make a blatant military march out of the recruiting song and the song of Jenufa. You instilled into it the glow of young hearts. "Every couple must endure its sorrow". Everywhere they made it into a funeral dirge, in Prague and even in Vienna. You gave it a smile and that is how it should be.

And how many horrible gaps they made in the second act.

You built it up on classical lines. At the end of the work, in the hymn to love, one feels actual flames in your *stringendo*.

You work up magnificently all the endings. It is you who have at last made *Jenufa* appear great; not Prague nor Vienna. If I may ask you for something, it is : the introduction to the first act, just a little quicker to give it an appearance of restlessness. And place the xylophone on the stage near the mill where its icy tone will be damped. That is all.

Well, let me thank you very much. Please give my regards to the gentlemen of the orchestra and my greetings to the best "Kostelnička" that I ever heard and to the other soloists and to the chorus.

I shall write to Mr. von Schillings separately.

As a matter of fact, I have arrived in Brno rather unwell. With best wishes,

Yours thankfully,

Leoš Janáček.

Brno, 22nd March, 1924.

A letter to *Erich Kleiber* (1890), who conducted *Jenufa* in Berlin: first performance 17th March, 1924.

189. *JENUFA* IN NEW YORK

As for *Jenufa* I have never seen such a setting and never heard such soloists and chorus. The way Jeritza sang and acted was a feast both for ear and eye. The climax was the "Kostelnička" of Madame Matzenauer. Such singing and acting. It must be seen and heard to be believed. During the second act I wept like a child. What heart-rending music ("Take her, Števa") and then the climax, — "Do you weep?" What an amount of feeling, it almost tears one's heart out. In many places I did not like the orchestra and the tempi; for instance, the beginning was overdone. The chorus, when singing "All get married", was too fast and lacked our Slavonic intensive rhythm.

I heard *Jenufa* twice, the first performance in New York and later in Philadelphia where I have a subscription ticket. In Philadelphia I spoke to Bodenzky. He sends you his greetings and he is very pleased to be conducting the opera.

28th February 1925.

From a letter written by *František Rybka*, Janáček's pupil, who attended the performances of *Jenufa* in New York and Philadelphia. — *Maria Jeritza*, a native of Brno, sang Jenufa in Vienna in 1919 and at the Metropolitan opera in New York first performance, 6th December, 1924. — *Artur Bodanzky* (1877—1940), conductor and pupil of Gustav Mahler, was active from 1916 at the Metropolitan opera in New York.

190. *JENUFA* TO BE PRODUCED IN ANTWERP

Dear Mr. Janáček,

I arrived in Prague only a few days ago, which explains my delay in answering your letter. In the first place I must give you the good news that Mr. Ebel, the head of the department and my chief, has received official information from the Antwerp opera house that *Jenufa* will be produced there this season.

In Berlin I had a talk with Schillings, who is also looking forward to the production of *Jenufa*.

I will send my essays on *Káťa Kabanová* to Mr. Wolfsohn in Cologne, whose letter you sent on to me.

Otherwise, I am in a rather bad situation and in a bad mood owing to the fall of the Reichsmark. Let us hope for better days. Kindest regards and best wishes.

Yours,

Max Brod.

3 1st August 1922.

The first performance of *Jenufa* in Antwerp took place in April 1927. — *František Ebe* (1881—1940), head of the press-department in Prague. *Max Schillings* (1868—1933), business-manager of the Berlin opera house. — *Julius Wolfsohn* (1880), German composer and pianist.

191. MILÉN'S DRAWING OF JANÁČEK

Dear Friend,

I saw my head in the office of Director Neumann.
I asked who did it.
I was told: You.
Dr. Brod has written to me that M. Prunières who publishes *Revue Musicale*, wants to bring out a number concerning my person and asks for a portrait, which should be a work of a r t.

I should like to send him your drawing. Have you got a copy of the one Neumann has at the theatre?

With best wishes,

Leoš Janáček, Ph. D.

Brno, 16th October, 1925.

Janáček's letter to the painter *Eduard Milén* in Brno. — There are many Czech artists who have portrayed Janáček in their various ways, e. g. painters: Dr. Desiderius (Hugo Boettinger), Cyril Bouda, Karel Svolinský, František Ondrúšek, Ondřej Sekora etc., sculptors: Emil Hlavica, Jan Štursa, Karel Pokorný. One of the best painters to have painted Janáček is Professor *Eduard Milén* (1891), a pupil of Max Švabinský, author of six drawings of Janáček. — *Henri Prunières* (1886), French musicologist.

192. EACH COMPOSER IN HIS OWN SUN

Sirs,

I am resigning the chairmanship of the Moravian Composers' Club. The time when I was needed has passed and each one of you is ripening in his own sun. I shall naturally remain an ordinary member of the Club.

With kindest regards

Leoš Janáček, Ph. D.

Brno, 13th November, 1925.

A letter to *František Neumann*. — The Moravian Composers' Club was founded in the autumn of 1922 and was mainly frequented by Janáček's pupils: Jan Kunc, Vilém Petrželka, Václav Kaprál, Jaroslav Kvapil, Osvald Chlubna, Josef Blatný, Břetislav Bakala and others. Janáček was the chairman from its founding until 1925. Neumann was, at the time, its vice-chairman.

193. REMINISCENCES OF YOUTH

Reminiscences of youth and the happier moments of life at the monastery foundation are expressed in Janáček's suite for wind sextet, *Youth*, 1924. The typical vamped rhythm which appears in the first part of the suite gives to the whole of *Youth* a flavour of wit and humour. The second part is meant to be a reminiscence of the unhappy moments in the isolation of the foundation under the restraint of strict regulations. The fourth movement, in quick tempo, combines the motives of the first and fourth part and is by its chromatic layout the most dramatic and effective of the movements. The third part is the original march of the Blue Boys showing how the Blue Boys of the 17th and 18th centuries in Brno used to whistle. Besides the typical vamped rhythm

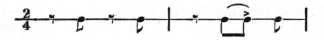

181

yet another interesting trait is to be found in Janáček's *Youth;* the use of unaccompanied solo instruments. Here Janáček probably had in mind the solos played by the boys of the foundation and reflecting the farcical circumstances of their environment. These solos are more richly ornamented than is usual in Janáček's melodies especially with turns, accented passing-notes and his much used trill and "sčasovky"—short, lively, rhythmical elements which ripple the calm melodic surface and are typical of Janáček's style.

In the same group of Janáček's reminiscences of his youth or even childhood, we find his *Nursery Rhymes.* A friend of children, the explorer of their speech and of the melodic curves of the child's language, Janáček found in the *Nursery Rhymes* a new creative impetus. He was won over by the gay note of the rhymes which in his transcription reach their culmination in the wit and humour of the sextet *Youth.* He wrote them during his summer holidays in 1925. On the 30th July, 1925 he writes to Mrs. Stössel: "I am setting nursery rhythms to music, it will be fun".

> Little Tommy Weatherway
> Took the goats to graze one day,
> But passing by the river-bed
> They jumped into the stream instead

and so on—something to laugh at. Do you know any more of such nonsense?

From my essay, *Janáček's Intimate Letters*, which was published in the magazine, *Hudební Rozhledy*, 1953.

194. AGAINST JAZZ MUSIC AT THE VENICE FESTIVAL

A town where the kings should live; especially the kings of the spirit. And they did live in Venice. The mighty sea narrows into the Grand Canal. Before leaving it again its white foam becomes

petrified into marble encrustations, slender pillars, smiling sta-
tues and symbolic figures on the palaces lining the banks of the water. I like these festivals of modern music. Twenty-eight composers
and twenty-eight compositions. All of them different. There was
more will to compose than there were explosive ideas; and more
of these than of art. Most of the good will was squandered on trivial
music. In my whole life I have never heard a more vulgar and more
theoretically helpless composition than the Daniel Jazz by Louis
Gruenberg. Let me tell you if you do not already know it that music of this kind cannot proclaim either love or hatred or sadness or
gaiety. Music can laugh, but with such laughter as this, it cannot force
others to laugh. There is no joke in it, no irony, no satire, no humour,
no joviality, no burlesque, no persiflage, no travesty nor masquer-
ade—and trivial music is now so much sought after.

From Janáček's article entitled *Duslu* which was reproduced by *Jan Racek* and *Leoš Fir-
kušný* in *Lidové Noviny*. It deals with the music performed at the third festival of the International
Society for Contemporary Music in Venice which Janáček attended (from the 3rd to the 8th
October, 1925). During this festival Janáček's *String Quartet* (1923), inspired by Tolstoi's *Kreutzer
Sonata* was performed. — *Louis Gruenberg* (1883), American composer of Russian descent

195. AGAINST COMMENTATING HIS WORKS

Sir,

I read your story about myself in the train. My worst enemy
could not have done it better.

1. First of all, I presume I am a Czech composer and not only
a *Moravian* one as they nowadays like to pretend in Prague.

2. I was Professor of Composition for the master-class of the
Conservatoire in Prague and not in Brno.

3. I am a Doctor of Philosophy of the Masaryk University
in Brno, and not of the Charles University in Prague.

4. After having studied the musical side of the language, I am
certain that all melodic and rhythmical mysteries of music in general

are to be explained solely from rhythmical and melodic points of view on the basis of the melodic curves of speech. No one can become an opera composer who has not studied living speech. I wish that this could be understood once and for all. I have studied this and am therefore able to compose dramatic music—that is to say, opera.

5. Is it therefore understood that this attitude is detrimental to my instrumental works? Therefore the Quartet is bad, *Youth*, the Violin Sonata, the Concertino—all that London has chosen is therefore bad?

6. I proclaimed freedom in harmonic progressions long before Debussy, and really do not need French impressionism.

Please see that all this is put right immediately. That is why I am writing to you at once tonight.

With kindest regards,

Yours,

Leoš Janáček, Ph. D.

Brno, 18th April, 1926.

To *Jan Mikota*. Janáček's reaction to a distorted biography of himself, published in the Riemann-Einstein *Musiklexikon*. He wrote the letter before his trip to England which lasted from 28th April to 10th May, 1926.

196. JANÁČEK IN ENGLAND

On the 30th April, 1936 a short notice appeared in *The Times*: Mrs. Rosa Newmarch is giving a small reception this afternoon at Claridge's to welcome the Czechoslovak composer, Dr Leoš Janáček.

Mrs. Newmarch was a friend of our nation. She had been to Czechoslovakia several times, where she met Czech artists and took a special fancy to the works of Leoš Janáček.

Janáček was, after Dvořák, the first Czech composer to be invited to England to attend performances of his works.

Under the auspices of Mrs. Newmarch, a committee of prominent musicians was formed in London which was to look after Janáček while in England. She first organised a small party to which she invited British artists, publishers and critics to meet Janáček who was, however, anxious about the issue. Would the invited guests appear? The day before he had been met at the station by the Czechoslovak ambassador, Jan Masaryk, and by Czechs living in London. But these were all countrymen. Now he had to make his appearance among the British.

All went well. There were so many guests, and Janáček received so many invitations, that he would have had to stay at least a fortnight in London in order to see everyone. On Sunday 2nd May, Mr. Henry Wood took him by car to his country house.

Janáček devoted himself to the preparations for his concert with his whole soul. He did not miss a single rehearsal and the British artists, on hearing his explanations, came to like his works still more. The programme of the concert consisted of the String Quartet (1923), Sonata for violin and piano (1921), *Youth* a suite for six wind instruments, and the *Fairy-tale* for violoncello and piano (1910). The success was very great and the public, with enthusiastic applause, called the composer many times on to the platform.

From an article by *Jan Mikota* who accompanied Janáček on his trip to England, 28th April — 8th May, 1926, published in the magazine *Hudební Besídka*, Vol. III, 1926. — *Rosa Newmarch* (1857—1940), British writer on music who played a part in introducing modern Czech music into England.

197. SUCCEEDS IN HIS MISSION

My dear Mrs. Stössel,

Should I continue living as I do now, I would certainly be dead within a month. Nothing but parties, food and sailing around in cars all day long. There is a strike here. The Londoners almost went without milk this morning. Prices are soaring. It is a bad atmosphere for a concert. But I have suceeded well in my mission. I have made many friends and found a patron who will see to it that *Jenufa* will be performed within a year. Now it will be better if I return home, otherwise I feel that I might never get away from here.

Yours very sincerely,

Leoš Janáček, Ph. D.

London, 5th May, 1926.

A letter to his friend *Mrs. Kamila Stössel*. — The strike referred to was the general strike of 1926.

198. A SHORT DREAM

My dear Mrs. Stössel,

Here I am again in Prague. Soon I shall be in Brno and all will seem to have been nothing but a dream. And yet, what preparations and anxieties it cost me. It is so simple to write something which neither disturbs nor hurts. Unfortunately in the turmoil of life, it seems rather s u p e r f l u o u s whether London, or rather that tiny bit of London, heard my works or not. This fact will change nothing in the course of events. Not even in the lives of a single one of its 8,000,000 inhabitants. In short, I am aware of the insignificance of musical work. There is no point in so much discussion of it. Others, on the contrary, take it too seriously; to these I do not belong. And that is that.

From Janáček's letter to his friend written in Prague on the 13th May, 1926.

199. BACK IN PRAGUE

The hall is well filled but not packed out. We are seated, contrary to all custom, around tables. And there at the head of the largest table, among young people, is a lively, agile man of seventy with merry sharp eyes. His high, arched forehead is crowned with a thick silvery mane. He talks and gesticulates so vehemenently that one becomes afraid that his old-fashioned cuff might fly off. Some important personality approaches the guest to welcome him from his successful tour. The guest rises: "Gentlemen, I feel as though I was living in a fairy tale... I went to London like Simple Simon and suddenly I find myself returning like a prince..."

Written by *Dr Jan Löwenbach* in the almanach entitled *Seventy Years of the Umělecká Beseda, 1863—1933*, p. 188.

200. SUGGESTIONS ON INTERPRETATIONS

Dear Madam,

It is now certain that I will not be going to Berlin to hear the concert. Rehearsals for the *Makropulos Secret* have started in Brno, and my presence is needed there. You will therefore have to take the responsibility of the Berlin success on yourself. One more remark; in the first movement of the violin sonata, the fiddle has, at one place, long, sustained notes, marked *piano*. The London violinist, Fachiri, gave these notes such intensive feeling, as though a restless soul were seeking peace, and the piano followed her in those *crescendos* and *decrescendos*; the section gained by it. Do it the same way. I know it would be enjoyable to go to Berlin, but here it is more urgent. Do let me know immediately after the first rehearsal how they play it. And one more thing: I do not know if you are going to play something from the *Mists* at the Legation. If so, then play two movements, not one by itself. The contrast makes a better effect.

With best wishes to you and your husband,

Leoš Janáček, Ph. D.

Brno, 28th November, 1926.

Madam,

The long notes on the violin which I mentioned are probably in the second movement (the Ballad).

Best wishes,

Leoš Janáček, Ph. D.

Janáček's letter and postcard to *Mrs. Ilona Štěpán—Kurz* before her Berlin Concert which took place at the begining of December, 1926. — *Ilona Štěpán—Kurz*, Czech pianist, the wife of the pianist, Dr.Václav Štěpán. She was famous for her excellent renderings of Janáček's works. — *The Violin Sonata* was composed during the years 1913 and 1921. — *In the Mists*, four piano pieces published in 1912,.

201. THE OPERA *THE MAKROPULOS SECRET*

I put *Fox Sharpears* behind me. And now what next? Whatever destiny brings. Life, I want life. It was at the Štrbské Pleso that I read Šalda's *Child*—everyone was praising it—and also *Makropulos*. I was caught by it. You know that terrible and sensitive thing in man, which is without end. Sheer misfortune. He neither wants nor expects anything. This had to be made into a work. The third act, that is what I am proud of. What speed, what development. That is what I felt, that is what I wanted. I worked on it about a year. I carried it in my head, pondered—but then, how the writing went forward like a machine.

Janáček composed the *Makropulos Secret*, after a play by Karel Čapek, in 1923—1925. — *František Xaver Šalda* (1867—1937), author and critic, wrote his play *The Child*, in 1923. — *Štrbské Pleso*, a mountain resort in the High Tatras.

202. COMPASSION FOR MANKIND

I have finished the *Makropulos Secret*. Poor 300 year-old beauty! People took her for a thief, for a liar, for a heartless animal. They called her beast, slut, they wanted to strangle her; and her fault? That she was doomed to live too long a time. I was sorry for her. Three years work is at an end. What now?

Brno, 5th December, 1925.

From a letter to *Mrs. Kamila Stössel.*

203. A REMARK ON THE PRODUCTION

Dear Friend,

One unusual chord can save a composition if the chord is a real bleeding knot of feeling. Your idea of the projected shadow in the second act brought the mystery of Emilie Marta to unexpected heights. Thank you for your work on the *Makropulos Secret*. But especially for this idea. You have greatly helped the work.

Yours sincerely,

Leoš Janáček Ph. D.

Brno, 24th December, 1926.

A letter to the Brno stage director, *Ota Zítek*, written after the first performance of Janáček's *Makropulos Secret* (18th December, 1926). — *Ota Zítek*, Czech composer, writer and stage director, who worked, in collaboration with the conductor František Neumann, on the Brno premiére of Janáček's operas, in particular *Šárka*, both the *Excursions of Mr. Brouček*, *Fox Sharpears* and the *Makropulos Secret*.

204. ČAPEK'S MODESTY

To Leoš Janáček, Ph. D., author of the *Makropulos Secret*, National Theatre

Dear Sir,

I wish with all my heart that tonight may once again be the occasion for your having a great success. I shall come to one of the performances in order to applaud your great work which I had the honour to inspire in a small way.
Yours very sincerely,

Karel Čapek.

A letter written on the day of the first performance of the *Makropulos Secret* in Prague (1st March, 1928).

205. CELEBRATIONS AT HIS BIRTHPLACE

Perhaps there has never before been such a celebration at Hukvaldy, the village under the ruins of the one-time mightiest Moravian castle, as on Sunday, 11th July, 1926. Neither bad weather, mud nor rain succeeded in spoiling the occasion at which the whole neighbourhood foregathered. Hukvaldy was celebrating the fame of one of its natives, the composer Leoš Janáček, and the unveiling of his memorial plaque.

The celebrations began on Saturday with two concerts of Janáček's compositions; one in Hukvaldy and one in nearby Kopřivnice where the workers' choral society elected Leoš Janáček their first honorary member.

The main celebration was on Sunday. For reasons of bad weather the chief events could not be held in front of the house where Janáček was born as had been originally planned, but had to be transferred to the village concert hall. The workers' choral society from Kopřivnice inaugurated the proceedings with Smetana's *Dedication*, after which the Mayor of Hukvaldy welcomed all those present, especially Mr. Janáček and the guests of honour. The director, Andrejs of Příbor then addressed the gathering. Janáček replied in the following words:

"When one has heard so much about oneself, it is difficult to believe that it could all be true. Some of it I am ready to accept, but a good deal of it I do not even want to hear. It is said that I have achieved something.

I have written a thing which was liked in southern, western and northern Bohemia, which was liked in Prague and in Moravia and Slovakia. And it occurred to me to ask myself what actually is the power of art? There is something in it, a sort of vibrating string which sounds everywhere and links us together wherever we may be.

Let us be grateful that it binds us and enables us to be strong, defiant and steady in the face of everything we encounter.

How did it all start with me? Even as a child I did not want to sit at home, I strove to get out; to be free as a bird; to go into the world and learn there. At liberty one grows up with a very different outlook from that of the narrow circle of home. I insist that young people do not sit at home; go out into the world!

I would never have thought that on the house where I was born would one day be a plaque commemorating that event. I never look back, only forward. You should all do the same. And you will be as happy as I am today."

From an article by *Josef Gregor* on the Janáček celebrations at Hukvaldy, published in the magazine *Hudební Besídka*, Vol. III, 1926—1927, p. 20. — *The memorial plaque* on the house where Janáček was born was unveiled on the 11th July, 1926. It is marble with a bronze relief of Janáček and bears the inscription: *To the genius of Czech music, Ph. D. Leoš Janáček, born in this house on the 3rd July, 1854.*

206. FOR THE BEST REPRESENTATION
OF CZECH MUSIC

Dear Madam,

By the same post I am writing to Mr. Hába and to the "Hudební Matice". It is you whom I want to play at Frankfurt, and the clarinet should be played by the gentleman from Brno. Here are my reasons:

1. Czech music must be represented perfectly.
2. You interpret the piano part in just the way I want it done. The clarinet part is difficult and was played best in Brno.
3. To play it well, rehearsals are necessary—and this will be a difficulty in Frankfurt.
4. Two instrumentalists should arrive there fully prepared. This is a guarantee of success.

I have written all this to Mr. Hába. I am also writing to "Hudební Matice" to forward my letters to him. It would be a good thing if you transmitted the contents of this letter to Mr. Mikota.

On my last visit to Prague I was incognito. I wandered about alone. Next time I shall visit you.

With best wishes to you and your husband,

Leoš Janáček, Ph. D.

Brno, 19th January, 1927.

A letter to *Mrs. Ilona Štěpán-Kurz* written in Prague before a concert of Janáček's compositions at Frankfurt. — *Alois Hába* (1893) was at that time propagating quarter-tone music, and was a member of the International Jury of the Society for Contemporary Music. — *Václav Mikota* was director of the Hudební Matice in Prague. — The clarinet in the Concertino played at Frankfurt was the Brno professor Stanislav Krtička (1887).

207. AT THE FRANKFURT FESTIVAL

In my class-room No. 8, at the Minorite Monastery, I often received a visit from Leoš Janáček, who used to come in the

23. Dr. Vladimír Helfert (1886—1945), Professor of Musicology at the Masaryk University in Brno, first important biographer of Janáček.

24. Janáček's grave in the Brno Central Cemetery.

evening and play me his w̶o̶r̶k̶s̶ and discuss with me whether this or that could be written for a certain instrument and what would suit it technically. In this class-room the piano resounded under his touch when he first played the score of his newly finished quartet, *Intimate Letters*. He put such temperament and force into his playing that his hands began bleeding from the knocks which he gave them on the keys. The fervour and endeavour to render accurately the ideas of his genius prevented him from noticing the wounds until he became aware of the blood stains.

During one such evening visit to the Minorite Monastery, Janáček briefly declared: "Here you have 140 crowns which I got from the Ministry for my trip to Frankfurt-on-Main. Come with me to the Festival and play my Concertino with Ilonka Kurz. Someone must come who knows the work. The people there would not be able to play it with only one rehearsal."

So I went, and with me went the clarinetist Stanislav Krtička whom Janáček took along for reasons of greater safety. As there was a musical exhibition at the Festival, Janáček persuaded the Ministry to send his favourite Myjava band to play folk music in national costumes.

In Frankfurt the Concertino was allotted a single rehearsal which took place on the morning of the concert, as it was impossible for members of the Theatre orchestra to be released from their rush of orchestral rehearsals. Janáček attended the rehearsal with Dr Václav Štěpán who had arrived with Ilonka. The nervous tension was strained as the members of the orchestra were completely exhausted by constant rehearsing for the festival, and showed no inclination for serious work. They obviously under-estimated Janáček's work and, not being aware of the special demands imposed on each single player, imagined that it would suffice just to play the work through. The apparent simplicity of the parts, which they had probably looked at only superficially, led them to presume that there would be no difficulties.

We started rehearsing. The viola player was comfortably seated next to me with his legs crossed and a cigarette hanging out of his mouth. He smoked away, and here and there even played a few notes. The others were no better. After the first few bars Janáček suddenly jumped up, rushed at the unfortunate viola player and began: "Well, dear sir, what on earth do you think you are playing? What are you dreaming about?" He stamped, shouted, and sang the parts as they should sound and the amazed viola player tried, with constant repetitions of a single typical Janáček figure, to perpetrate an unknown style, until the cigarette fell out of his mouth and he lost all desire for further smoking.

His colleagues watched the scene with wide eyes. I began to expect a stormy quarrel. But the German players were, as I soon found out, excellent artists and saw with their flair for musicianship that there was "someone" standing in front of them.

During the performance, all the composers whose works were played waited nervously behind the scenes in order to run on to the stage immediately their compositions ended, so as to catch their applause. Only Janáček sat among the public in the stalls of the theatre where the concert was taking place. After the great success of his work, it was from there that he stood up to acknowledge the thunderous applause. His beautiful, impressive grey head attracted and surprised the audience. Under the influence of what they had just heard, they had expected a young hot-head. The success was even carried out into the street when Janáček threaded his way from the Theatre through a throng of Dutchmen, Englishmen and Germans, all applauding with enthusiasm.

From a letter written by *František Kudláček* (1894—), leader of the Moravian Quartet and professor of the Janáček Academy of music and dramatic art.

208. IN ŠEVČÍK'S TOWN

From 1924, Janáček became a frequent visitor to the town of Písek and took a lively part in the local cultural life. Janáček never missed any important occasion even if it did not concern music. We all liked him very much and it was a red-letter day for Písek musicians when he arrived. Ševčík's pupils played his compositions with great interest and later made them still more known abroad. Janáček always came to Písek whenever anything of his was being played. Písek was, in the years 1924 till 1928, perhaps the only provincial town in Bohemia where Janáček was performed regularly and with success. The second String Quartet, *Intimate Letters*, was performed in Písek shortly after its Brno première; *The Diary of One who Vanished* was given twice, the first time by local artists. It was in Písek that Janáček was inspired to write his Military Symphonietta, while sitting in the park listening to a concert of a military band.

Janáček used to tell us with enthusiam about his symphonic poem, *The Danube* and often played extracts from it on the piano.

These are only fragmentary reminiscences from the great Písek days of Janáček and Ševčík.

Extract from a letter which was sent to me by *Cyril Vymetal* (1890), one of the leading members of the musical life of Písek, at that time professor of the Písek High School of forestry. — Pupils of the famous violin teacher *Otakar Ševčík* formed the *Lipkin Quartet* (1852—1934) and played Janáček's first *String Quartet* in Písek on the 8th September, 1927. — *The second String Quartet* was written by Janáček between the 29th January and the 19th February 1928 at Hukvaldy and Brno. The original title of this quartet, *Love Letters*, later changed to *Intimate Letters*, allows us to guess his sentimental attachment to Písek, the town where his friend *Mrs. Kamila Stössel* was living. This work was first performed by the Moravian Quartet in Brno (František Kudláček, Josef Jedlička, Josef Trkan, and Josef Křenek) on the 11th September, 1928. The second performance took place in Písek, for the first time by local artists, on the 2nd May, 1925.

209. CONCERT WITHOUT CELEBRATIONS

Dear Sir,

I thank you for your kind invitation. I wonder how you have coped with the difficult programme. I am on my way to Prague for the rehearsals of *Fox Sharpears*. I shall come down and visit you. I would ask of you just one thing: let the concert be an ordinary concert without any celebrations of my person whatever.

This is my urgent desire.

I shall arrive on Friday at 3 p. m.

Yours very truly,

Leoš Janáček, Ph. D.

Brno, 29th April 1925.

A letter to *Cyril Vymetal* who invited Janáček to a concert of his compositions which took place in Písek on 2nd May, 1925. The programme included the *Violin Sonata*, the *Diary of One who Vanished* and *Lachian Dances*. Janáček was present. — At that time rehearsals of *Fox Sharpears* were in progress in Prague and this seventh of his operas, after its first performance in Brno in 1924, had its premiére in Prague on the 18th May, 1925.

210. *INTIMATE LETTERS* IN PÍSEK

Dear Sir,

Today they played me my second Quartet, *Intimate Letters*. The Moravian Quartet played it brilliantly. Their fee should be increased to include the 3rd class fare from Brno to Písek and back.

It is a trip which would take them two days.

I would not care to see the whole evening filled up with my works only. It would be an inadmissible imposition on you, which would be unforgivable.

How will you cover your expenses?

You could enliven the programme by the playing of young Firkušný. He could play after Dvořák's Quartet, then again, with Mr. Kudláček, my Violin Sonata, and after that would come the Second Quartet. I know you want Firkušný for a separate concert with the orchestra. A concert of chamber music, however, would be a good introduction for him and what is most important, the Sonata would need no rehearsing. I could have a word with Firkušný and see to his fee.

I will ask Mrs. Stössel to give a lunch for the gentlemen if there is no mourning in the family – her mother is gravely ill.

She might even invite two or three of the gentlemen to stay in her house. The Quartet will also be writing to you. I wish you a good holiday.

Yours sincerely,

Leoš Janáček, Ph. D.

Brno, 27th June, 1928.

Janáček's last letter to professor *Cyril Vymetal* in Písek. — The *Second String Quartet*, see previous remarks. — *Rudolf Firkušný* (1912), famous Czech pianist, did not appear at the above mentioned concert.

211. JANÁČEK'S *SYMPHONIETTA*

In the *Symphonietta* the character of the motives and the way they are worked out is something of a surprise. From the technical point of view, all the typical Janáček traits—the sparkling invention, passionate temperament and the changing rhythm and metric qualities—appear in this work in unprecedented balance. There is ardent temperament, but no explosiveness. If I did not want to be contradictory, I would say that Janáček here approaches some kind of a classical period in his development. Here are none of his excited, obstinate interjections, which used to burst into the musical structure of his former works, preventing them from developing for lack of space. Instead of that we find a firm, logical continuity of musical thought, which assumes supremacy to the end of the work. An architectural monument such as this has not before appeared so emphatically in Janáček's music. And this no doubt is the consequence of the fact that the composer did not allow himself to be attracted by literary and illustrative ideas, but kept to the laws of purely musical construction. Janáček's *Symphonietta* represents what was for him a new orchestral style in the sense of pure musical architecture and balance of expression.

Janáček's untiring and ever fresh spirit gave new proof of his indomitable strength and creative power.

From Helfert's essay *Janáček's Symphonietta*, which was published in the new edition of Helfert's essays on Janáček, Prague 1949. — Janáček sometimes called this work *Military Symphonietta*. He completed it on the 1st April, 1926 and dedicated it to Mrs. Rosa Newmarch.

212. GLAGOLIC MASS

Old Slavonic mass. You know, what they wrote about me: "The old man who believes in God". This made me cross, and I said: "Young man, in the first place, I am not old, and a believer in God not at all; no, not at all". Until I had found out the opposite. It just struck me that this year, 1928, is lacking something. The atmosphere of St. Methodius is missing and I wanted to add something to it with my work. I have had the work finished since 1926. The idea came to me in Luhačovice. A dreadful time; it rained day after day and every evening I sat down, took my bearings and started off. In three weeks it was done. I wanted to portray the faith in the certainty of the nation, not on a religious basis but on a basis of moral strength which takes God for witness.

From Janáček's interview which was published in the magazine *Literární svět*, Vol. I, 1928. For further information on Janáček's holidays in Luhačovice, see my essay entitled *Leoš Janáček and Luhačovice* (Luhačovice 1939). — The words *the old man who believes in God* were written about Janáček by Dr. Ludvík Kundera (1891), the present rector of the Janáček Academy of Music and Dramatic Art.

213. THE OPERA *THE HOUSE OF THE DEAD*

Janáček, while pursuing his way as an artist, was bound to feel drawn towards Dostoevsky because he was a poet whose extensive literary message contained strong dramatic tension, rebelliousness and opposition to the laws of God and humanity. The creator of the *Brothers Karamazov*, the *Adolescent*, the *Idiot, Crime and Punishment*, could scarcely pass by Janáček's creative spirit without arousing a very distinct echo. It is surprising that Janáček chose the *House of the Dead*. The intensive humanity of Dostoevsky in his *House of the Dead* made such a strong aesthetic impression on Janáček that without considering whether it was dramatic or undramatic, he threw his whole spirit into the artistic work which was nearest to him, viz. opera, in which he reaches down to the most wretched. He wrote the following motto on the score. "In every creature is a spark of God". In this lies the entire ethical power and magnificence of the idea behind the work which is also a picture of Janáček's artistic personality. Janáček read Dostoevsky's books in the original. He was too great a Russophile to be satisfied with a mere Czech translation. Already, while reading through the work, he had a clear picture of the scene as presented in music.

In it Janáček created a new type of opera, a collective opera, over which rings out one idea, common to both Janáček and Dostoevsky — compassion for the poor and the wretched.

The expression of this compassion is the true ethos of Janáček's work; its great moral strength never disappears even in the most destitute for "in all creation there is a spark of God".

From *Leoš Firkušný's* book, *The Message of Leoš Janáček to Czech Opera*, Brno, 1939

214. HOW JANÁČEK LIVED

The house behind the Conservatoire into which Janáček moved on the 1st July, 1910, was one of the nicest houses in Brno. Certainly, a more convenient place for the director of the organ school and the creator of *Jenufa* to live in could scarcely have been found. Besides the living arrangements inside the house, which Janáček influenced very considerably, the situation of the house compared with the other buildings must also be taken into consideration. In fact, this advantage was especially great as it gave the impression of a quiet, over-sized still-life, protected from the south by the Conservatoire, from the north by the large building of the old Seminary, and open only on the side facing Smetana street.

After Janáček had left his post of director of the organ school, he rose early in summer, but in winter was awakened somewhat later by the noise of the fire being lighted in the stove. In summer he breakfasted on a bright, sunny veranda which he loved almost as much as his study. In winter he breakfasted in his wifes' bedroom which was next to his study. He came down to breakfast in an old house-suit and spent a long time reading thoroughly the paper "Lidové Noviny". If there were criticisms or articles on his works, he would pass the paper to his wife for her to read aloud. He worked every day until 11 o'clock. After work he went for a walk or strolled to the station to fetch the post. In the afternoon, he again sat down to composing. At five o'clock he stopped work and walked over the Špilberk hill, although in winter he preferred the park or a stroll through the town where he might make some purchases. Soon after six he would be home again waiting hungrily for dinner. After dinner he liked to sit with his wife on the veranda or, if the weather was fine, in the garden. The hour before he retired to bed he devoted to his correspondence. Then he slept— well and healthily—disturbed only occasionally by his lively musical dreams.

215. LOVE OF ANIMALS

His love for animals was one of his typical characteristics. So much did he love them that it made them, with the possible exception of the pigeons, which Janáček kept on the roof of the conservatoire, react in quite an unusual way. He made pets of the hens because they laid him so many eggs. He taught them to jump up at his order on to the garden table when it was time for them to go to roost. And from there they were carried to the attic where they had their hen-house. He used to go for walks with them round the garden. He taught them not to scratch in the flower-beds and behaved to them altogether in a much more friendly way than is usual with hens. Both his dogs, the black, sturdy poodle called Čert, and the mongrel, Čipera, were eccentrics. Janáček spent much time entertaining himself in this animal society and made use of it for his musical studies. He used to listen attentively to the song of his gold finch. He noted down the change in Čipera's bark when he was no longer a puppy. He walked about the garden with him and when they met a black, furry caterpillar, and Čipera growled with surprise, he quickly took down his growl.

From an article by *Dr Robert Smetana* (1904—), author of the book, *Stories about Janáček* (Olomouc 1948).

216. LOVE OF NATURE

Janáček loved nature perhaps more than anything else. Whoever saw him gardening and watching intently the growth of all God's creatures, could only envy him his satisfaction and happiness. Cowslips, snowdrops, violets gave him no end of pleasure and he could not bear his garden to be without them. His greatest joy used to be caused by pairs of warblers and blackbirds when they came to nest in his garden. He followed them about and became quite absorbed when watching them rearing their young. Blackbirds were his speciality. Bent, almost on his knees, he would follow their performances and the feeding of their young and their first efforts at flying. Someone, out of spite, let a lizard and a frog loose in his garden. When I suggested that he should get rid of them he answered: "What an idea! I am glad to have them here..."

From an article by *Osvald Chlubna, Reminiscence of Leoš Janáček*, published in the magazine *Divadelní Listy*, Vol. VII, Brno 1931—1932.

217. HABITS WHILE COMPOSING

Zdeňka knows very well when I am working; both she and Máňa are afraid to enter my room. When I am working, the entry of anyone whatever, under any kind of circumstance, means that I must get up. I cannot stand even an importunate fly, flying about the room. Unexpected steps or rustling in the next room disturb me. Disturb me! I would burst out in anger, I would be nasty, unbearable. In creative work it is like that—I tell you quite openly; like a mother who is about to give birth and is prevented. The natural process is choked. As though some one was stopping your mouth so as to prevent you from breathing. As though the earth was about to give way under your feet.

I know that Zdeňka suffers under all this. But I warned her before she took the step. She brought her father to Brno without sufficient consideration. Her father, who has a son that is certainly more close to him. I also had a mother. Poor, destitute—and she was not able to live with me. It is not a question of her father, it is a question of me and my living arrangements, my activities, my work, of all my such very modest happiness, my domestic peace and quiet which I have built up with such difficulty. It is not a question of physical comfort, it is my spiritual balance which is at stake.

14th February, 1921.

A letter from Leoš Janáček to his friend *Mrs. Kamila Stössel.* — *Zdeňka Janáček* (died 1938), Janáček's wife. — *Máňa Stejskal*, general help in the Janáček household.

218. SUDDEN DEATH

Janáček left here for the last time on Monday, 30th July, 1928, some time before 10 o'clock in the morning, to catch the train to Přerov which he always took when travelling to Hukvaldy.

A few days later—12th August 1928—the postman delivered two telegrams. The first announced that he had suddenly been taken dangerously ill, the second announced his death.

From an article by *Robert Smetana*.

219. THE FUNERAL

Few in number were those who had found out that, on this August day, the body of Leoš Janáček would be lying in state in the church of Old Brno . . . In one of the adjoining chapels of the church which stood wide open, lay, on a low catafalque, a dark brown coffin with the lid removed. In it lay a second coffin with a glass top. The loneliness was oppressive. In the dusk, nothing could be seen at first except the small white hands, folded together and holding a cross. So small, like the hands of a woman. Not until you came nearer could you make out the lines of his beautiful head with its high forehead, bushy eyebrows and typically protruding chin which gave the face its energetic expression. Tightly closed eyelids, a bitter smile on his closed lips. Why was there no plaster cast made of his face, or at least, of his hands? Here in these surroundings began his life's pilgrimage, as a boy—and now here it had come to an end. He, under whose fingers the organ rang out with such new, unusual magic. It is strange; no-one enters. At least, no-one disturbs the living image. The living image of Janáček's abrupt speech with its Lachian accent, his queer, rocking gait and his gestures. How hard to believe he is dead, he that breathed life into so many works. From outside comes the sound of life which will go on. And now, it is as though the music has suddenly sounded from somewhere. Perhaps it is the sigh of Maryčka Magdonová or the whine of Sharpears, or is it Amarus praying? Káťa, Jenufa,

Taras Bulba—all appear before us. Yet there is no one here. On the coffin a bunch of white roses lies at the feet of the dead in thanks for all the youth and beauty to which he gave his heart.

From an article by the poet, *Jaroslav Vyplel* (1890—), who wrote several poems on Janáček. The article appeared in *Lidové Noviny* on the 12th August, 1938.

220. OBITUARY SPEECH

The Czech Academy of Science and Art loses with your sudden death one of its most valuable and most famous members, who enlightened the life of the Academy for over sixteen years. Your personality was the perfect prototype of a member who was able to combine the officialdom of his great cultural significance with the freedom and revolutionary spirit of creation and who, until his old age, managed to stay young and fresh in spirit, over-flowing with a joyful will towards new artistic achievements. Sir, your spirit departs for the Kingdom of God and your body returns to the earth of your motherland. Your artistic message and the remembrance of the genius and the usefulness of your spirit will remain with us for ever.

From the speech which *Dr Boleslav Vomáčka* (Czech composer, born 1887) delivered as representative of the Czech Academy of Science and Art in Prague. It was printed by *Adolf E. Vašek* in his book *In the Footsteps of Dr Leoš Janáček* (p. 207).

221. TALICH ON JANÁČEK

That was a head. Beautiful, hard, self-assertive, obstinate. A tough nut! That is why Janáček could wait his time. That is why he had such a sense of the dramatic value of the pause. What was

Brno like forty years ago when *Jenufa* came into being? But the spirit hovered over the wilderness and the spirit prevailed. What can be a better example for our contemporary impatience?

From *Václav Talich's* article *In Connection with Jenufa* which appeared in the magazine *Eva*, Vol. XIII, No. 6, 1941, pp. 6—7. — The outstanding Czech conductor, *Václav Talich* (born 1883), was for many years director of the Czech Philharmonic Orchestra of which he is now artistic adviser. He is especially known for his exemplary performances of Janáček's operas and for his renderings of Janáček's symphonic works.

222. THE SO-CALLED ECCENTRIC

When Janáček first began to be known in Prague he seemed to us to be something of a Diogenes. Some one whose opinions on art differed from those of the majority of artists, some one who refused to acknowledge the fundamental norms of musical technique. Tales of this unusual Moravian musician were such that if some one had stated for a fact that he lived in a tumbledown hut and fed himself on forest plants and made his own clothes and shoes, we would almost have believed it. He appeared to us so completely isolated and so purposefully contemptuous of culture. Life for him became bearable only when he was among Moravians. Only occasionally were we given the chance of finding out something of his enormous treasury of Moravian and Slovakian folk songs, of his knowledge of ethnography, of his studies in Moravian dialect and of his theories of speech melody.

It was only in his later life that *Jenufa* suddenly showed us the strength of this original Diogenes among musicians. It then became clear that the creator of *Jenufa* was no ordinary being. Suk, Hoffmann, Talich and we younger ones, were absolutely won over by the newness and strength of Janáček's music. Now also, the long years of Janáček's life were revived. Works appeared of which the main incentive was obviously Nature, works which drew their sap from the roots of the earth; the roots of Moravia. And added to all this, a strong personality who could penetrate into the depths and essence of huma　entities. A musician had appeared whose art was the music of the　ood and roots of human substance.

From *Ota Zítek's* articl　itten on the occasion of Janáček's seventieth birthday celebrations which appeared in *Lido　Noviny* on the 3rd July, 1924 under the title *With a Bouquet in the Hand*. — The Czech composer *Josef Suk* (1874—1935) was for many years a member of the famous Bohemian Quartet. — *Karel Hoffmann* (1872—1936), former first violin of the Bohemian Quartet and professor at the Prague Conservatoire.

223. A DEEPLY COMPASSIONATE ARTIST

Janáček was a deeply compassionate artist. Even in this was something Eastern. The bright optimism of Smetana cannot be found in his music, only the uplifting clarification of the catharsis. Probably all people of his type suffer or are unhappy, and Janáček is able to take them in his arms with a gentle hand, which caresses them lovingly and brings them salvation. *Jenufa* is a work of great love and compassion. The most distressing, although most famous of his life's works, which brought him so much sorrow and later so much fame. Similarly in *Maryčka Magdonová*, *Kantor Halfar*, *The 70,000* we hear the tones of great love, humiliated and insulted, with which Janáček ranks himself among the true creators of to-day. Janáček loves even the unhappy Káťa Kabanová. Like her, he is filled with fervent passion, suffering and longing. A beautiful work of unhappy love. This is one of the marks of Janáček's music—passion—an almost erotic passion. In the years when others have finished with creative work and with life, this grey eagle is in love with passionate life, filled with sorrowful longing. Janáček's last work, *Intimate Letters*, clearly demonstrates this. Let us love Janáček because he suffered so much. We honour his moral strength and the sincerity of his art. He trod to the end a thorny path. Proudly and incorruptibly, until he reached his goal. A great personality—with his national art he reached international status.

Dr *Emil Axman* (1887—1949), Czech composer and author, extolled Janáček's personality in an obituary article published by the Czech Academy of Art and Science (Almanach Vol. XXXIX, 1929, pp. 156, 161 ff.).

224. JANÁČEK AND NOVÁK

I met Janáček in Brno at the time when he was still on friendly terms with Reissig. Naturally within a few minutes, we were arguing hotly over the way the folk song "Listen, listen" in the Sušil collection, had been written out. Janáček approved of it. I did not, because it is evident that the rhythm should alternate between 2/4 and 3/4 time. I also discovered—apart from this weakness—his artistic intolerance and that his acquaintance with music in general was limited. This was the reason why I made a point of avoiding the subject of music in my later meetings with him, always excepting the village music of Hukvaldy. I visited him there twice, on both occasions staying for several weeks. Once, when we were out walking, he wrote down a few words from a conversation which he had with an old woman—it was his so-called speech melodies and was taken down just at the time when he was writing *Jenufa*. But I found out about these circumstances only later. When, after the Prague premiére of the opera, he suddenly leapt into fame, I was one of his most sincere well-wishers especially because of all the insults he had suffered. I never resented his attacks on my "Tempest" or "Sonata Eroica", although my attention was always being drawn to them. We got on very well together, especially as these attacks were simply part of his character . . .

From a letter to me from *Vítězslav Novák* (1870—1949), Czech composer, written on the 4th November 1940. — Janáček and Novák were acquainted with each other from the year 1897, when Novák first visited Brno. In August of the same year they played Novák's *Three Czech Dances* for piano duet at Janáček's birthplace, Hukvaldy. On the 20th March, 1898, Janáček performed *The Neighbours Dance* from the suite at a concert of the Czech orchestra in Brno. Novák dedicated his second collection of *Songs on Moravian Folk Poetry, op. 17*, to Janáček. Novák's *Sonata Eroica* for piano was first performed in Brno in the year 1905. — *František Sušil* (1804—1868), collector of folk songs. His most famous collection was published in 1835.

225. CONSTANT STRIVING FOR ORIGINALITY

I have no particular memory of Janáček but I remember that my father who was one of his teachers often said that Janáček was by far his best and most contemplative, although a permanently dissatisfied, pupil. (My father counted his pupils by the thousands). If he resolved a dissonance in a certain way, he immediately wanted to know if it could be used in the reverse way. That is to say, if it was an ascending resolution, he asked if it would not be possible to make of it a descending resolution. In this he continued to be interested even in his old age, a young hot-head, as is generally known.

From a letter from *Josef Bohuslav Foerster* to me (14th November 1940). *My father: Josef Foerster* (1833—1907), father of Josef Bohuslav Foerster, composer and professor at the Prague Conservatoire. Janáček was not directly his pupil but was examined by him when taking his State Examinations in piano and in organ playing. (1875).

226. A CZECH CLASSIC

On the 28th January, 1925 I was present at the confering of the degree on Janáček. I will never forget the beautiful ceremony and the soft serious expression in the eyes of the composer, who was and will remain our greatest modernist because his music is new deep-felt and unusually arresting. In the recognition of Janáček, I see the recognition of Czech music. Smetana, Dvořák and Janáček are the fundamental pillars of Czech creative music. We respect them and we may be thankful that they are fully recognised, not only at home but also by the whole world. Let us not say that Czech music has reached its high-water mark. We wish for a further proud and healthy expansion, just as Smetana, Dvořák and Janáček would have wished, naturally an expansion such as they deserve.

An excerpt from the speech which *Josef Suk* (seep.172) made on the occasion of his receiving an honorary degree at the Masaryk University in Brno in 1934, published in the magazine *Tempo — Listy Hudební Matice*, Vol. XIII, 1933—1934, p. 135.

25. Leoš Janáček (A drawing by Eduard Milén).

227. GATEWAY TO CONTEMPORARY DRAMATIC MUSIC

I wish to see Janáček established in the National Theatre in such a way as his genius deserves, whether we compare him with our dramatic composers of the past or with those of the future; and as far as the future is concerned, I consider it my most important duty to popularize Janáček because he is the gateway leading to contemporary dramatic music.

From an article by *Václav Talich* (see p. 205), *Our Duty to Popularize Janáček*, which appeared in the paper *Národní listy* on the 19th February, 1941 at the time when Talich was director of the Opera at the National Theatre in Prague (1935—1945).

228. AGAINST TRADITION

In a time of groping and uncertainty, old Janáček comes to the fore, a primitive genius. He creates from inspiration and when we compare him with his older and younger contemporaries, seems to go out of his way to be as simple as possible. He was daring enough to say what he thought! A thing which in itself makes a strong impression even if one does not necessarily speak the truth. He repudiated all so-called tradition, and paid little attention to what was going on around him in the world of art. He went his own way. He did not recognise even the highest authority. Sometimes he made provocative criticism of even the very greatest composers—Beethoven and Smetana. In this and also in the emphasis he laid on folk art, he resembles Stravinsky. On the other hand, he appreciated, oddly enough "Verists" (for example Puccini) and even allowed himself to be influenced occasionally by them. If we can say that he grew out of any of our masters, then it is only Dvořák. Naturally, only from the point of view of musical invention. The structure of his works has much in common with Fibich although one could scarcely say that he was influenced by him.

From *Otakar Jeremiáš's* (1892—) essay *Leoš Janáček*, Prague, 1938.

229. A BORN DRAMATIST

The endless quick pulse of life beats in his works, there is continuous excitement. This is why his works do not ease, they flay us. Maybe they are not liked—maybe this is why they arouse so much opposition—but they never leave anyone unmoved. The constant aspiration of life, a sense of external action pushing on, defines his dramatic spirit. Janáček is a born dramatist. Not in vain was he driven all his life to compose operas. All his working methods are predestined directly to opera, especially his plasticity and his primitiveness. His dramatic sense is apparent in his other works also. Take his choral works, they are not mere lyrical effusions, they are indeed dramatic scenes—full of the truth of life which have the power almost to tear out our hearts. We see the action as if it were taking place before our eyes.

Ludvík Kundera, rector of the Janáček Academy of Music and Dramatic Art (b. 1891).

230. AN ARDENT RUSSOPHILE

Mussorgsky also began his development from the intonation of speech, but when he had passed the period in which his music was submitted to these theories *(The Marriage)*, he reached a point where he developed a consequent melodic style in which the intonation of speech signifies only the starting point for great realistic melody *(Khovanshchina)*. Janáček, on the contrary, as far as I can judge, did not go so far as to elaborate, from the intonations of speech, a vivid, melodic line, and for this reason the declamatory character prevails over the fully-fledged melody. Contemporary Czechoslovak composers probably cannot avoid the musical experiences of popular speech intonation which were gathered together by Janáček. But it would be wrong for them to persist. For only true melody, which grows out of the seeds of popular speech, can become the basis of true, realistic musical language.

We are especially interested in Janáček's works in which he manifests his sympathy for Russia. We have only to point out that this was the incentive for his rhapsody Taras Bulba (1915—1916), a very interesting work which is played throughout the Soviet Union. Janáček wrote: "Not because he beat his own son to death for having betrayed his country, and not because of the martyr's death of his second son, but because there were no flames and tortures which could break the power of the Russian people. For these words uttered by the famous Cossack leader, Taras Bulba, as he was being burned at the stake, I have composed this rhapsody after the legend retold by Gogol." Thus, in Janáček's work, are expressed the love and sympathy which have always existed between the peoples of Czechoslovakia and of Russia.

From the article by *Dmitri Kabalevsky* (1904), which appeared in the magazine *Music of the Soviet Union*. In 1950 it was translated into Czech and published under the title *Remarks on Music in Czechoslovakia* (in the magazine *Music of the Soviet Union*, 1950).

231. RESEMBLANCE TO MUSSORGSKY

In the same way as Mussorgsky, Janáček attracts me by his warm interest in every living creature. The more humble the creature, the more his sympathy is aroused. This sympathy was extended even to dumb animals. This is not mere imitation of Mussorgsky—they have something in common. They both make "vivid conversations with people" and tell "the truth, even to the smallest detail".— Do not be afraid. Do not steal. No one took these maxims more literally to heart. I have studied other composers longer and more uninterruptedly, but if I think of Janáček, I think especially of the wrongs which he suffered. We suspected him of disorderliness, and ignorance even of the basic principles of composition and orchestration, which he succeeded in defending and reinstating only in *Káťa Kabanová*. As if such a musician would not immediately be able to hear the current technical machinations if he had wanted to!

From *Jaroslav Křička's* (see p. 139), article on *Janáček's Choral Works* printed in the magazine *Listy Hudební Matice*, Vol. IV, 1924—1925, pp. XII and ff.

232. THE TEACHER OF TRUTH AND HONESTY IN MUSIC

Leoš Janáček prepared me for a musician's life with great thoroughness. With his firm, experienced, and yet kindly hand, he guided me through all the jungles and labyrinths of music and knew how to lead a small child to an interest in musical theory and composition, how to advise him in piano playing and give the incentive for study in general. He demanded of us a good education and was himself one of the best educated of the Czech composers. He adapted himself to me and looked for the path along which a child could go without the danger of an accident. It was not an easy task to explain to a five-year-old child the principles and truths of music, keep him to his work and make the lessons interesting and enjoyable, and to see that he conscientiously fulfilled the task which he had undertaken. He did not keep to any known educational formulas. He created his own methods according to the pupils' individuality and never forgot that he was handling the intellect of a child... He understood a child's naiveté, but in his contact with the child he could maintain almost the same relations as with an adult. He taught children with the help of his own childish characteristics. He reckoned with the child's inability to concentrate and pay attention, but he was also able to arouse in them the seriousness of a grown-up person, when the question of music was under discussion. In spite of his fiery temper, in spite of his composing activities and his other valuable artistic and social work, he never showed any impatience in his lessons. On the contrary, he often extended them, and never underestimated even the most insignificant of my exercises in music, and never made me aware of his adult authority. He had his own inimitable methods of awakening love of music, and the way he could interest, never over-praising, but at the same time sounding the most sensitive strings of the child's heart, was truly great. Among his many educational methods was his taking me to his box to hear the Brno premières of his operas. Today I can still recall the excitement, deep respect and great admiration combined with my own great pride, when I heard, sitting close to my master, the first performances of his *Káťa Kabanová*, *Fox Sharpears* and the *Makropulos Secret*. Not until I had grown up was I able to understand what precious seeds he had sown in my child's mind.

From an article by *Rudolf Firkušný* (1912—), well known Czech pianist, which appeared in *Lidové Noviny* on the 12th August, 1938.

233. IGOR BELZA ON JANÁČEK

Till the last days of his life, Janáček never ceased to love the Russian people. In 1918, when the bourgeoisie of the whole world rose against the young Soviet Republic, Janáček was finishing his orchestral rhapsody, *Taras Bulba*, based on the story by Gogol. In the score of *Taras* are to be found elements of decadent expressionism. They appear in the complexity of the harmonic progressions, in the sharpness of the dynamic contrasts and in the unmelodiousness of the intervals. But at the same time, we find in the rhapsody realistic episodes in effect unveiling a picture of the powerful Russian people, which the composer himself considered to be the leading idea. That is why the ideological and artistic value of the rhapsody is given mainly by this conception of heroic patriotism, which is underlined with sufficient decision to enable the expressionist elements which penetrate into the later works of Janáček to be pushed into the background.

No doubt, it is the tradition of realism which Janáček followed when choosing his subject that contributed so much to the success of his struggle against the flow of Western modernism, which gained such ground in the Czech music of the first third of the twentieth century.

From the book by the Soviet musicologist, *Igor Belza: Očerki razvitija češskoj muzikaľnoj klassiki* (Moscow, 1951).

234. THE JANÁČEK ARCHIVES IN BRNO

Janáček, as the creator of new values in the field of Czech spiritual culture in Brno before the first World War, was among the foremost of those whose work prepared the ground for the emergence of Brno as a second cultural centre which crystallized in the founding of the Czech University. His sincere and lasting interest in the Faculty of Arts is proved by the following circumstance: When I became a lecturer at the University, Janáček was professor of the master-class in composition. On his own impulse he arranged with me that I should fix my lectures at such a time as would enable his own students to attend them. He also laid great stress on the importance of their attending my lectures. The legacy which he left in his will to the Faculty of Arts of the Masaryk University was the result of these circumstances of which naturally his honorary doctorate was for him the most pleasing.

To this legacy was added the gift of Mrs. Janáček who, according to her husband's will, gave to the Faculty of Arts his entire correspondence beginning in 1879, his note-books, sketches, collections of criticisms, articles published in various magazines and daily papers etc. Also, the text books from his library which contain his numerous and extremely valuable marginal notes. Also, his many

hitherto unpublished works, as well as many which were then unknown, were made accessible, together with new editions of his
works.

On account of this generosity and, in the history of Czech
music an isolated example, Janáček's Archives were assembled in
the Faculty of Arts of the Masaryk University and in this way was
founded a memorial of Janáček the scholar.

From an article written by *V. Helfert, The Gathering Together of Janáček's Inheritance·*
Newly published in the collection of Helfert's *Essays on Janáček*, Prague, 1949.

235. THE TREASURE OF OUR ART

In his works I hear as much of Moravia as I do of Bohemia
in the compositions of Smetana. I consider them to be a great musical record of Moravia. Janáček belonged, and in fact still belongs, to
our day. He is a modern even if we do not take into account his
interesting technical experiments. But he is more than merely modern: his place is incorruptibly and irrevocably among the unper-
ishable t r e a s u r e s   o f   C z e c h   a r t.

From the magazine, *Rytmus*, Vol. VIII. — Author of this quotation, *Dr Albert Pražák*,
professor at the Prague University and one of the leaders of the 1945 revolution in Prague.

This catalogue is divided into groups of various types of compositions, drawn up according to my alphabetic catalogue of Janáček's works. (Opava 1952, Silesian Research Institute.) Unfinished works have been omitted. Each composition bears its title and states for what it was written. In brackets are added the author of the words, the year of composition, latest edition (where published, when, by whom) and gramophone recordings. If the composition is unpublished, a note has been added to indicate that it is in manuscript. This systematic catalogue of Janáček's compositions and arrangements was prepared according to the following layout:

A. VOCAL MUSIC

    I. FOLK SONGS
        1. Collections and Bouquets of folk songs
        2. Arrangements for piano with words
        3. Arrangements for solo voice and piano
        4. Arrangements for choir (beginning from duets)
           a) women's choir with or without accompaniment
           b) male voice choir with or without accompaniment
           c) mixed choir with or without accompaniment

    II. SONGS (WITH ACCOMPANIMENT)

    III. MELODRAMA

    IV. CHORAL WORKS
        1. women's choir
        2. male voice choir
        3. mixed choir

    V. MASS AND REQUIEM

    VI. CANTATAS

    VII. DRAMATIC MUSIC
        1. Incidental music
        2. Ballet and pantomime
        3. Opera

B. INSTRUMENTAL MUSIC

    I. SOLO INSTRUMENTS
        1. Piano
           a) Dances
           b) Variations

A. VOCAL MUSIC

Translations of Czech words stated separately

I. FOLK SONGS

1. Collections and bouquets of folk songs

1. *František Bartoš Leoš Janáček:* A Bouquet of Moravian, Slovakian and Czech National Songs. *(Kytice z národních písní moravských, slovenských i českých.)* (1890, Prague, 1953 State Publishing House KLHU. IV. edition. Alltogether 195 songs.)
2. *František Bartoš:* Moravian National Songs newly collected. *(Národní písně moravské nově nasbírané.)* Musical editor Leoš Janáček. (Prague 1901, Czech Academy of Science and Art.) Comprises Janáček's essay on Moravian national songs (p. 141). Musical edition of 2057 songs of which 47 were collected by Janáček himself in Wallachia and Lachia.
3. *Leoš Janáček—Pavel Váša:* Moravian Love-Songs I. *(Moravské písně milostné I.)* (Prague 1930, Orbis. 150 songs and many variants.)

2. Arrangements for piano and organ

1. *Ten Czech Religious Songs* from Lehner's Hymn-book *(Deset českých církevních zpěvů z Lehnerova mešního kancionálu.)* (1881, Brno before 1889, Karel Winkler, II. edition.)
2. *Moravian Folk Songs* for piano. *(Moravské lidové písně pro klavír.)* 15 folk songs with their words. (1922, Prague 1950, Hudební Matice).
3. *Christ is born. (Narodil se Kristus Pán.)* Czech Christmas carol for piano with words. (In the magazine "Hudební Besídka", III, 1926, 66.)

3. Arrangements for solo voice and piano

(Complete cycles and *not* individual songs stated).

1. *The little Queens. (Královničky.)* 11 folk songs. (1889, Prague, 1954, State Publishing House KLHU.)
2. *Moravian Folk Poetry in Songs. (Moravská lidová poesie v písních.)* 53 folk songs. (About 1892 and 1901, Prague 1947, Hudební Matice. Partly on Supraphon records.)
3. *The Folk Poetry of Hukvaldy in Songs. (Ukvalská lidová poesie v písních.)* 13 folk songs. (1898, Prague 1949, Hudební Matice, III. edition. Recorded by Supraphon.)
4. *Six National Songs* as sung by Eva Gabel. *(Šest národních písní, jež zpívala Gabel Eva.)* (About 1909. 1. volume, 26 folk ballads. Prague 1950, Hudební Matice.) German translation by Max Brod.
5. *Songs of Dětva. (Písně dětvanské.)* (Bandit ballads.) 3. vol. 26 folk ballads, 8 Slovak songs (1916, Prague 1950, Hudební Matice).
6. *Silesian Songs. (Slezské písně.)* 10 folk songs from the collections of Helena Salich. (1918, Prague 1954, State Publishing House KLHU, 2nd edition.)

4. Arrangements for choir

a) Women's voices with piano

Folk Nocturnes. (Lidová nokturna.) Slovak nocturnes from Rovné. 7 Folk duets. (Before May 1906. Prague 1950, Hudební Matice. 2. vol., 26 folk ballads. Recorded by Supraphon.)

b) Male voices, with or without accompaniment

Five National Songs for male voice choir and solo with piano or harmonium. *(Pět národních písní pro mužský hlas a sbor.)* (1916—1917, Prague 1950, Hudební Matice, 4. vol., 26 folk ballads.)

c) Mixed choir

Songs of Hukvaldy. 6 folk songs. (1899, Prague 1949, Hudební Matice.)

II. SONGS (with piano)

1. Spring Song. *(Jarní píseň.)* (Jaroslav Tichý, 1897, Brno 1944, Oldřich Pazdírek. Recorded by Supraphon.)
2. *The Diary of One who Vanished. (Zápisník zmizelého.)* For contralto and tenor (No. IX, X) and 3 women's voices with piano accompaniment. (1919) To words by an unknown poet (Prague 1953, 2nd edition, State Publishing House KLHU. German translation by Max Brod, French translation by Hanuš Jelínek and Daniel Müller. Recorded by Supraphon.)
3. *Nursery Rhymes.(Říkadla.)* 19 Rhymes. (Vienna 1928. Universal Edition. Recorded by Supraphon.)

III. MELODRAMA

Death. (Smrt.) (Lermontov, 1876.) With orchestral accompaniment. Lost.

IV. CHORAL WORKS

1. Women's choir

1. *Songs of Hradčany. (Hradčanské písničky.)* Cycle of 3 songs with accompaniment. (František S. Procházka, 1916, Prague, 1922, Hudební Matice. Recorded by Supraphon.)

2. *Kašpar Rucký.* Ballad for women's choir with soprano solo. (František S. Procházka, 1916; Prague 1938, Hudební Matice, 2nd edition. Recorded by Supraphon.)
3. *The Wolves' Footprints. (Vlčí stopa.)* With piano accompaniment. (Jaroslav Vrchlický, 1916, in manuscript.)

2. Male Voice Choir

1. *Fickle love. (Nestálost lásky.)* (Folk poetry, 1873. In manuscript.)
2. *Song of War. (Válečná.)* For piano, trumpet and 3 trombones. (1873. In manuscript.)
3. *Four Male-voice Choruses. (Čtyři lidové mužské sbory.)* (Eliška Krásnohorská and folk poetry. 1873, 1893, 1914. Prague 1948, Hudební Matice, 3rd edition. Recorded by Supraphon.)
4. *Lonely without Consolation. (Osamělá bez těchy.)* (Folk poetry, 1874. In manuscript.)
5. *Rest. (Odpočiň si.)* (František Sušil, 1875, Prague 1926, Hudební matice. Recorded by Supraphon.)
6. *In folk song style. (Ohlas národních písní.)* 3 choruses. (Folk poetry, 1876, Prague 1937, Melpa. Recorded by Supraphon.)
7. *Ballad. (Zpěvná duma.)* (František Ladislav Čelakovský, 1876, in manuscript.)
8. *No escape from Destiny. (Osudu neujdeš.)* (Folk poetry, 1878, in manuscript.)
9. *The Jealous Lover. (Žárlivec.)* With baritone solo. (Folk poetry, 1888, in manuscript.)
10. *The Sun has risen over the woods. (Už je slunko z tej hory ven.)* With tenor solo. (Folk poetry cca 1894.)
11. *Festival chorus. (Slavnostní sbor.)* (Vladimír Šťastný, 1897. In manuscript.)
12. *Veni Sancte Spiritus.* (Religious poetry, cca. 1900. In manuscript.)
13. *Constitues.* With organ accompaniment. (1903. In manuscript.)
14. *Four Moravian male-voice choruses. (Čtvero mužských sborů moravských.)* (Ondřej Přikryl and folk poetry, 1904, Prague 1950, 2nd edition, No. 3 and 4. German edition Leipzig 1908, R. Forberg in his collection "Männerchöre aus dem Repertoire des Sängerbundes mährischer Lehrer". German translation W. Henzen. Recorded by Supraphon.)
15. *Kantor Halfar.* (Petr Bezruč, 1906. Prague 1948, 2nd edition, Recorded by Supraphon.)
16. *Maryčka Magdonová.* (Petr Bezruč, 1906—1907. Prague 1950, 3rd edition. Recorded by Ultraphon.)
17. *The Seventy Thousand. (Sedmdesát tisíc.)* (Petr Bezruč, 1909. Prague 1929, Hudební Matice. Recorded by Supraphon.)
18. *The Czech Legion. (Česká legie.)* (Antonín Horák, 1918. In manuscript. Recorded by Supraphon.)
19. *The Wandering Madman (Potulný šílenec.)* With soprano solo. (Rabindranath Tagore 1922. Prague 1925, Hudební Matice. Recorded by Supraphon.)
20. *Our Banner. (Naše vlajka.)* With 2 solo sopranos. (František S. Procházka, 1926. In manuscript.)
21. *Chorus for the laying of the foundation stone of the Masaryk University. (Sbor při kladení základního kamene Masarykovy university.)* (Antonín Trýb, 1928. In manuscript.)
22. *Four male-voice choruses. (Čtveřice mužských sborů.)* (Jaroslav Tichý and folk poetry. Before 1885. Prague 1948. Hudební Matice, 3rd edition. German translation Max Brod. Recorded by Supraphon.)

3. Mixed Choir

1. *Festival chorus. (Slavnostní sbor.)* With piano. (Karel Kučera, 1877. In manuscript.)
2. *Regnum Mundi.* (1878. In manuscript.)
3. *Three mixed choruses. (Tři smíšené sbory.)* (Jaroslav Vrchlický, Svatopluk Čech and folk poetry 1880, 1885, 1890. Prague 1950, Orbis.)
4. *I was sowing... (Zelené sem sela.)* With orchestra. (Cca 1892. In manuscript.)
5. *Elegy on the death of his daughter Olga. (Elegie na smrt dcery Olgy.)* With piano. (M. N. Veverica. 1903. In manuscript.)
6. *When we went to the feast. (Keď zme šli na hody.)* Highland dance with orchestra. (In manuscript.)

V. MASSES

1. *Mass* after Liszt's Messe pour Orgue. Arranged by Leoš Janáček for mixed choir and organ. (1901. In manuscript.)
2. *Mass in E flat Major* for mixed choir and organ. (1908. Only Kyrie, part of the Credo and Agnus. The Credo was completed and scored by Vilém Petrželka. In manuscript.)
3. *Glagolic Mass. (Glagolská mše.)* (See cantatas.)

VI. CANTATAS

1. *Kyrie. (Hospodine, pomiluj ny!)* For solo quartet and mixed double-choir, with organ, harp, 3 trumpets, 3 trombones and 2 tubas. (1896. In manuscript.)
2. *Amarus.* Lyrical cantata for solos, mixed choir and orchestra. (Jaroslav Vrchlický, cca 1897. Prague 1938, Hudební Matice. Full score and parts.)
3. *Our Father. (Otče náš.)* For tenor, mixed choir and piano or harmonium. Arranged for organ and harp accompaniment. (1901—1906. Originally as incidental music to tableaux-vivant after pictures by the painter Josef Krzesz-Męcina. In manuscript.)
4. *Čarták on the Soláň (Na Soláni čarták.)* For male-voice choir and orchestra. (M. Kunert, 1911. In manuscript.)
5. *Everlasting Gospel. (Věčné evangelium.)* A legend for solos, mixed choir and orchestra. (Jaroslav Vrchlický. 1914. In manuscript.)
6. *Glagolic Mass. (Glagolská mše.)* For solos, mixed choir and organ. 8 sections. (Miloš Weingart. 1926, Vienna 1928. Universal Edition. Vocal score. Recorded by Supraphon.)

VII. DRAMATIC MUSIC

1. Incidental music

Our Father. (Otče náš.) See cantatas. Originally incidental music to tableaux-vivant after the paintings of Josef Krzesz-Męcina. (1901. In manuscript).

2. Ballet and pantomime

Rákoš Rákoczy. Scenes from Moravian Slovakia with dances and songs in one act, 41 sections. (Lachian-Wallachian and Hanakian dances and folk songs arranged for solos and chorus with orchestra. Scenario by Jan Herben, ballet arranged by August Berger. 1891. In manuscript.)

3. Opera

Šárka. Opera in 3 acts. (Julius Zeyer. 1887. In manuscript.)
Beginning of a Romance. (Počátek románu.) One act. (Libretto Gabriela Preis and Jaroslav Tichý. 1891. In manuscript.)
Jenufa. (Její pastorkyňa.) Moravian musical drama in 3 acts. (Gabriela Preis. From 18th March 1894 to the 18th March 1903. Prague 1948, Hudební Matice. 5th edition. Recorded by Ultraphon. Fantasy on themes from the opera arranged for piano duet by B. Morlák. Vienna 1918, Universal Edition. Fantasy for light and small orchestra arranged by E. Bauer. Vienna 1927. Universal Edition. Vindobona Collection.)
Destiny. (Osud.) Opera in 3 scenes. (Libretto by Leoš Janáček, made into verse by Fedora Bartoš. 1904. In manuscript.)
The Excursions of Mr. Brouček. (Výlety pana Broučka.) Section I. Excursion of Mr. Brouček to the Moon. 2 acts. (Libretto Svatopluk Čech, adapted by Victor Dyk, Karel Mašek, Zikmund Janke, František Gellner, Jiří Mahen, Josef Holý and František S. Procházka. 1908—1917.)

Section II. Excursion of Mr. Brouček to the XVth century. 2 acts. (Libretto Svatopluk Čech, adapted by František S. Procházka. 1917. Vienna 1919. Universal Edition.)
Káťa Kabanová. Opera in 3 acts. (After the play by A. N. Ostrovsky *The Storm.* Translated by Vincenc Červinka. 1919—1921. Vienna 1922. Universal Edition.)
The Adventures of Fox Sharpears. (Příhody lišky Bystroušky.) Opera in 3 acts. (Rudolf Těsnohlídek. 1921—1923. Vienna 1924. Universal Edition. Some of it on Supraphon records.)
The Macropulos Secret. (Věc Makropulos.) Opera in 3 acts. (Karel Čapck. 1923—1925. Vienna 1926. Universal Edition. Some of it on Supraphon records.)
House of the Dead. (Z mrtvého domu.) Opera in 3 acts. (After the novel by Dostoievsky. 1927—1928. Vienna 1930. Universal Edition. German translation Max Brod.)

B. INSTRUMENTAL MUSIC

1. Solo instruments

1. Piano

a) Dances

Lachian Dances. (Lašské tance.) 6 orchestral dances arranged by Jindřich Máslo. Prague 1948, (Hudební Matice. 2nd edition.)
National Dances of Moravia. (Národní tance na Moravě.) 21 dances of which 12 are arranged for piano duet. (Collected and edited by Lucie Bakeš, Xavera Běhalek, Martin Zeman and Leoš Janáček. Cca 1891 and 1893. Prague 1953. State Publishing House KLHU. 2nd edition. Added are Two Moravian Dances: Pilky and Čeladenský.)
Ej, danaj! Slovak dance. (1892. In manuscript.)
Moravian dances. (Moravské tance.) Čeladenský and Pilky. (Cca 1904. Brno 1905. Arnošt Píša. Newly published in the National Dances of Moravia.)
Polka. (Krajcpolka.) (Cca 1912. Facsimile of the manuscript in the paper "Lidové Noviny".)

b) Variations

Variations. (1880. Prague 1944, Hudební Matice, under the title Thema con Variationi. Zdenka's Variations.)

c) Sonatas

"Sonata A Street Scene". (Z ulice.) "1. X. 1905." 15 pieces. 2 sections preserved: Foreboding and Death. (1905. Prague 1949, Hudební Matice, 2nd edition. Recorded by Ultraphon.)

d) Cycles of programme music

Music for gymnastic exercises. (Hudba ke kroužení kužely.) (Cca 1893, Prague 1950, Hudební Matice.)
Up the overgrown Path. (Po zarostlém chodníčku.) 7 pieces originally for harmonium. 15 pieces for piano. 1901—1908. (Prague 1947, Hudební Matice. 5th edition. Recorded by Ultraphon.)
In the Mists. (V mlhách.) 4 pieces (1912, Prague 1950, Hudební Matice.)

2. Solo instruments with accompaniment

1. Piano concerto and concert pieces

Concertino for piano and chamber orchestra. (2 violins, viola, clarinet, horn and bassoon. (1925. Prague 1949, Hudební Matice. 2nd edition. Recorded by Supraphon.)

Capriccio for piano with the left hand and chamber orchestra. (Piccolo, flute, 2 trumpets, 3 trombones and tenor tuba.) (1926. Prague 1953, State Publishing House KLHU. Recorded by Supraphon.)

2. Violin concerto

Violin concerto: Soul's pilgrimage. *(Putování dušičky.)* 1927—1928. Used as an introduction to the opera *House of the Dead.*

III. CHAMBER MUSIC

1. Duets

a) For piano

Dances etc.

Starodávný. The first Wallachian-Lachian dance. (Cca 1889. In manuscript.)
National Dances of Moravia. (Cca 1891 and 1893. 12 dances from the National Dances of Moravia.)
Introduction to Jenufa. (Jealousy.) *(Žárlivost.)* (1894. In manuscript.)

b) For violin and piano

Sonata

Sonata No. 3. (Cca 1913, 1921 in 4 movements. Prague 1947, Hudební Matice, 2nd edition. Recorded by Ultraphon.)

Concert pieces

Fourth Romance. (1879. Prague 1949, Hudební Matice. 2nd edition.)
Dumka. (1880. Prague 1945, Hudební Matice.)

c) For violoncello and piano

Presto. (Cca 1910. In manuscript.)
Fairy-tale. (Pohádka.) Inspired by the fairy-tale *Czar Berendei* by V. A. Zhukovsky. (1910, Prague 1949, Hudební Matice, 2nd edition. Recorded by Supraphon.)

2. Piano trio

Piano trio. Inspired by Tolstoi's "Kreutzer sonata". (1908—1909. Lost.)

3. String quartets

1st String Quartet. Inspired by Tolstoi's *Kreutzer Sonata* (1923. Prague 1948, Hudební Matice, Recorded by Supraphon.)
2nd String Quartet. Intimate Letters (Listy důvěrné) (1928. Prague 1949. Hudební Matice. Recorded by Supraphon.)

4. Wind sextet

Youth. (Mládí.) Suite for wind sextet. (1924, Prague 1947, Hudební Matice. Recorded by Supraphon.)

IV. ORCHESTRAL

1. Dances

Lachian Dances. (Lašské tance.) 6 dances. (1889—1890. Prague 1951. 2nd edition. Recorded by Supraphon.
Moravian Dances. (Moravské tance.) 6 dances. (Cca 1892. In manuscript. Recorded by Supraphon
Cossack Dance and Serbian Reel. (Kozáček a Srbské kolo.) 1899. In manuscript.

2. Overtures

Introduction to "Jenufa". (Jealousy.) (1894. In manuscript.)

3. Suites

Suite for string orchestra. (1877. 6 movements. Brno 1926. Oldřich Pazdírek. 4th section recorded by Supraphon.)
Idyll. 7 movements. (1878. Prague 1952. Orbis.)
Suite op. 3. Also called Serenade for full orchestra. (1891. In manuscript.)

4. Symphony, symphonietta

The Danube. (Dunaj.) Symphony in 4 movements. (1923—1928. In manuscript.)
Symphonietta. (1926. Vienna, Universal Edition 1927. Recorded by Ultraphon.)

5. Symphonic poems

The Fiddler's Child. (Šumařovo dítě.) Ballad for orchestra, after the poem by Svatopluk Čech. (1912. Prague 1949, 3rd edition.)
The Ballad of Blaník. (Balada blanická.) After the poem by Jaroslav Vrchlický. (1920. In manuscript.)
Taras Bulba. Rhapsody for orchestra after the story by Nikolai Gogol. (1918. Prague 1947. Recorded by Supraphon.)

BIBLIOGRAPHICAL INDEX
(In chronological order)
AUTOBIOGRAPHIES AND CORRESPONDENCE

Adolf Veselý: Leoš Janáček. Study of his works and life. Prague 1924.
Artuš Rektorys: Correspondence of Leoš Janáček and Artuš Rektorys. *(Korespondence L. Janáčka s Art. Rektorysem.)* Prague 1934, 2nd edition 1949.
— Correspondence of Leoš Janáček and Otakar Ostrčil. *(Korespondence L. Janáčka s Otakarem Ostrčilem.)* Prague 1948.
— Correspondence of Leoš Janáček and František S. Procházka. *(Korespondence L. Janáčka s F. S. Procházkou.)* Prague 1949.
— Correspondence of Leoš Janáček and Gabriela Horvátová. *(Korespondence L. Janáčka s Gabrielou Horvátovou.)* Prague 1950.
— Correspondence of Leoš Janáček and Karel Kovařovic and the Management of The National Theatre in Prague. *(Korespondence L. Janáčka s K. Kovařovicem a ředitelstvím Národního divadla v Praze.)* Prague 1950.
— Correspondence of Leoš Janáček with the librettists of The Excursions of Mr. Brouček. *(Korespondence L. Janáčka s libretisty Výletů Broučkových.)* Prague 1950.
Jan Racek and Artuš Rektorys: Correspondence of Leoš Janáček with Maria Calma and Dr František Veselý. *(Korespondence L. Janáčka s Marií Calmou a MUDr. Fr. Veselým.)* Prague 1951.
— Correspondence of Leoš Janáček and Max Brod. *(Korespondence L. Janáčka s Maxem Brodem).* Prague 1953.

JANÁČEK'S MOST IMPORTANT PUBLICATIONS

The Composing of chords and their modulations. *(O skladbě souzvuků a jejich spojů.)* Prague 1897.
Method of teaching singing. *(Návod pro vyučování zpěvu.)* Brno 1899.
Trends in Czech music. *(České proudy hudební.)* Brno, the magazine "Hlídka", 1897—1899. Analysis of Dvořák's symphonic poems, Fibich's operas *Šárka* and *Hedy*, Kovařovic's *Dogheads* etc.
On the music of Moravian national songs. *(O hudební stránce moravských národních písní.)* Prague 1901. In the collection of František Bartoš: Newly collected national songs of Moravia.
Complete textbook of harmony. *(Úplná nauka o harmonii.)* Brno 1912—1913. 2nd edition 1920.
Janáček's articles from the paper "Lidové Noviny". *(Janáčkovy feuilletony z Lidových Novin.)* Edited by Jan Racek and Leoš Firkušný. Brno 1938.
Essays on folk songs. *(Statě o lidové písni.)* Prague 1955. Edited by J. Vysloužil.

WRITINGS ON JANÁČEK

Jan Kunc: Leoš Janáček. In the magazine "Hudební Revue". Vol. 4. Prague 1911.
Max Brod: Leoš Janáček. Prague 1924. In German. Czech translation.
Rosa Newmarch: Leoš Janáček. In Groves' Dictionary of Music and Musicians. 3rd edition. 1927.
Emil Axman: Leoš Janáček. In the Almanach of the Czech Academy in Prague. 1929.

A. E. Vašek: In the Footsteps of Leoš Janáček. *(Po stopách L. Janáčka.)* Brno 1930.
Daniel Muller: Leoš Janáček, Paris 1930.
Leoš Firkušný: Leoš Janáček as Critic of the Brno Opera House. *(L. Janáček kritikem brněnské opery.)* Brno 1935.
Jan Racek: Leoš Janáček. Remarks on his personality as a creator. Olomouc 1938.
František Pala: Analyses of Janáček's operas *Jenufa, The Excursions of Mr. Brouček, Káťa Kabanová, The Adventures of Fox Sharpears, The Macropulos Secret* and *The House of the Dead.* Brno–Prague 1938.
Vladimír Helfert: Leoš Janáček. Vol. I. Brno 1939.
Bohumír Štědroň: Leoš Janáček in letters and reminiscences. *(L. Janáček v dopisech a vzpomínkách.)* Prague 1946. German translation: Artia 1955
Ludvík Kundera: Leoš Janáček and the Friends of Art Club. *(L. Janáček a Klub přátel umění.)* Olomouc 1948.
— Janáček's School of Organists. *(Janáčkova varhanická škola.)* Olomouc 1948.
Robert Smetana: Stories about Leoš Janáček. *(Vyprávění o L. Janáčkovi.)* Olomouc. 1948.
Jaroslav Vogel: Leoš Janáček the Dramatist. *(L. Janáček dramatik.)* Prague 1948.
Leoš Janáček. — A study of his life and works. *(Leoš Janáček — Obraz života a díla.)* Edited by Jan Racek. Brno 1948.
The Diary of One who Vanished. *(Zápisník zmizelého.)* Brno 1948. Essays by František Trávníček, Bohumír Štědroň etc.
Jaroslav Procházka: Lachian Roots in Janáček's Work (Prague 1948).
Vladimír Helfert: On Janáček. *(O Janáčkovi.)* A collection of essays and articles. Prague 1949.
Igor Belza: Očerki razvitija českoj muzikalnoj klassiky. (Moscow–Leningrad 1951.)
Bohumír Štědroň: Catalogue of Janáček's compositions and arrangements. *(Seznam Janáčkových skladeb a úprav.)* Opava 1952.
Bohumír Štědroň: Janáček's Jenufa. *(Janáčkova Její pastorkyňa.)* Prague 1954.
Musikologie III. Edited by J. Racek. Prague 1955.

b) to Janáček

LIST OF COMPOSITIONS SPOKEN ABOUT IN THE BOOK

LEOŠ JANÁČEK

Letters and Reminiscences

Dr Bohumír Štědroň

Translated from the Czech
by Geraldine Thomsen

Prague Czechoslovakia
Printed in Czechoslovakia